"*Feminist City* is a damning stab at the subtle and overt manipu-
lation of women in urban spaces. Kern's interwoven references
to her personal experience through childhood, adulthood, and
motherhood make her deeply researched and whip-smart work
infinitely readable. Kern shows that the ability of *all* women to
exploit the city fully is a valuable, necessary gauge for city worth."

—Lezlie Lowe, author of *No Place To Go:*
How Public Toilets Fail Our Private Needs

"How do we begin to reckon with and ultimately reimagine our
public realm in the #MeToo era? We can start by lifting up a
greater diversity of experiences and voices that influence our
thinking about what makes a place equitable, fun, accessible,
safe, and dynamic for all. Kern's exploration is honest, timely,
and intentional in acknowledging the work of women—fellow
urbanists and others—in advancing the feminist city."

—Lynn M. Ross, AICP, urban planner and feminist

"*Feminist City* is the next-generation urbanism book I've been
waiting for! Leslie lays out a comprehensive guide to feminist
world-building that our cities so desperately need. A must-read
for all city officials and budding urbanists alike as we move into
the female future of our urban environments."

—Katrina Johnston-Zimmerman, MUS, urban
anthropologist and adjunct professor, Lindy Institute
for Urban Innovation, Drexel University; co-founder
of The Women Led Cities Initiative

"Leslie Kern provides a refreshingly clear analysis of contemporary urban life. *Feminist City* seamlessly weaves together theory and lived experience, revealing again and again just how essential feminist geographic thought is to understanding urban space. *Feminist City* is a book to be shared and discussed by anyone who loves cities."

—Lauren Hudson, SolidarityNYC

"This volume definitively establishes Kern as a leading and impassioned voice in the second generation of North American feminist urban geography. Kern deftly and refreshingly interweaves her personal biographical narrative and a synthesis of feminist urban scholarship to capture the tensions between city-as-barrier and city-as-possibility that continue to infuse so many women's daily urban experiences."

—Damaris Rose, honorary professor of social geography and urban studies, Institut national de la recherche scientifique, Montreal, Quebec

"I wish I could have read this book years ago. The experiences Kern reflects upon are ubiquitous, if not universal. Kern blends the best of academic literature with popular culture references to explore the ways in which urban space is gendered. Reading the book is a pleasure, like a deep conversation with a wise friend."

—Winifred Curran, professor of geography, DePaul University

FEMINIST CITY

LESLIE KERN

VERSO
London • New York

This paperback edition published by Verso 2021
First published in Canada in 2019 by Between the Lines, Toronto, Canada
www.btlbooks.com

1 3 5 7 9 10 8 6 4 2

Verso
UK: 6 Meard Street, London W1F 0EG
US: 20 Jay Street, Suite 1010, Brooklyn, NY 11201
versobooks.com

Verso is the imprint of New Left Books

ISBN-13: 978-1-78873-982-5
ISBN-13: 978-1-78873-983-2 (UK EBK)
ISBN-13: 978-1-78873-984-9 (US EBK)

British Library Cataloguing in Publication Data
A catalogue record for this book is available from the British Library

Library of Congress Cataloging-in-Publication Data
A catalog record for this book is available from the Library of Congress

Design by Ingrid Paulson
Author photograph by Mitchel Raphael
Printed and bound by CPI Group (UK) Ltd, Croydon, CR0 4YY

For Maddy

CONTENTS

ACKNOWLEDGEMENTS

I'd like to thank everyone at Between the Lines Books and in particular my editor Amanda Crocker, for enthusiastically saying "yes" to this book and supporting me throughout the publication process. Leo Hollis at Verso has also played a critical role in finding opportunities for this book to reach as wide an audience as possible. Many people at Between the Lines and Verso have worked hard on this project, including Julia Judge, Maya Osborne, David Gray-Donald, Karina Palmitesta, Devin Clancy, Chelene Knight, and more.

I tend to keep my projects pretty close to my chest until they're nearly done (it's a Scorpio thing), but I want to thank those folks who gave me early encouragement and advice as I let the news trickle out: Erin Wunker, Dave Thomas, James McNevin, Caroline Kovesi, and Pamela Moss.

The fierce, creative, rigorous, and engaged community of feminist geographers has been my intellectual home for many years now and I could never do this work without *their* work. Our gatherings, conferences, and book parties are so meaningful to me. I've been especially lucky to have Heather McLean, Winifred Curran, Brenda Parker, Roberta Hawkins, Oona

Morrow, Karen Falconer Al Hindi, Tiffany Muller Myrdahl, Vannina Sztainbok, and Beverley Mullings as friends, co-authors, and collaborators.

My mentors and advisors from graduate school continue to inspire me and I'm grateful for everything they've done to help me succeed: Sherene Razack, Helen Lenskyj, Gerda Wekerle, and Linda Peake.

My colleagues and students at Mount Allison University have fostered a warm and invigorating environment for my work over the last twelve years. Special shout out to everyone who's ever taken *Gender, Culture, and the City*: this book is a pure distillation of what a particularly-engaged cohort once called "Kernography." Our conversations helped frame the goals for this book.

My urban and not-so-urban adventures have been filled with fun and sisterhood and travel and tattoos and cheese and impractical footwear because of my two girl gangs, the Pink Ladies of Toronto and the Sackville Lady Posse. In order of appearance in my life: Jennifer Kelly, Kris Weinkauf, Katherine Krupicz, Sarah Gray, Cristina Izquierdo, Michelle Mendes, Jane Dryden, Shelly Colette, and Lisa Dawn Hamilton. The west coast auxiliary includes the generous and vivacious Katie Haslett.

I've always had the unfailing support of my family, including my brother, Josh, and my parents, Dale and Ralph. My father passed away suddenly the day after this book was first published. His pre-ordered copy arrived too late for him to see it, but I know that he was proud of me and excited to hold the book in his hands. My partner, Peter, makes the coffee every morning, which basically allowed me to write every word of this book. My daughter Maddy is an absolute light. I love you all and deeply appreciate everything you do for me.

PREFACE

There's nothing like a crisis (or two, or three) to make crystal clear everything at stake in the worlds we imagine through projects like *Feminist City*. When I wrote the book, I embraced a care-full vision of the city. However, the turmoil of the last two years has pushed me to think and speak more concretely about both the effects of a care deficit in our cities and specific ways we can build care into the city at every level. I'm more convinced than ever that this framework is essential for our mutual survival in a crisis-torn century.

The Covid-19 pandemic illustrated just how badly we've neglected care infrastructures and how much we rely on the un- and under-paid labour of a feminized and racialized workforce to patch the gaps. The exploitative and unsustainable nature of this system was laid bare early in the pandemic, as the impossibility of sustaining "the economy" without the work that makes work and workers possible was exposed. Decades of progress toward gender equality in the home and workplace were rolled back in an instant.[1] The reliance of this progress on the backs of poorly-paid domestic- and child-care work was also highlighted. It became clear that success for some women has not been facilitated by men doing their fair share of care work. Rather, it's because that work has been passed on to an even more marginalized sector of the workforce, one that's been on the frontlines throughout this crisis.[2]

The scale of the "she-cession," as some have dubbed it,[3] as well as fear about declining birth rates as women resist having children in such precarious circumstances,[4] has shocked some governments into action. In Canada, the federal government included plans to develop a national child care system in its 2021 budget. In the United States, President Biden's 2021 infrastructure plan included care work as infrastructure that supports the economy as much as any bridge, road, or railway. Other places are promising "feminist recovery plans" to "encourage deep structural transition to an economy that better values the work we know is essential to sustaining us."[5]

Cities are critical sites for rethinking how and where care work happens. It's time to be innovative in housing design and think outside the patriarchal box of the single-family home, which hides so much undervalued labour and invisible violence. Co-housing, intergenerational housing, flexible construction, and of course affordability measures are needed to ensure a wider range of housing options for modern families and to pull more care work out of the home and off of women's exhausted shoulders. To this end, care work has to be a priority in the design of buildings, public spaces, transportation systems, and neighbourhoods. Cities can also mandate living wages, which would especially benefit women and racialized people who work in the underpaid service economy, often in care worker roles. A universal basic income would also go a long way toward ensuring that care work is valued, since it essentially provides a wage for caregivers.

The pandemic has also been a moment of reckoning for our decidedly-uncaring public spaces. As governments urged us to take our social lives outside, we found hardened, inhospitable environments with few places to sit, no shelter, no water, and no bathrooms. Plans to get people outside seemed to focus on allowing private businesses like restaurants to take over sidewalks for expanded outdoor service. This gives more public space over to the wealthy and takes it away from those who can't afford such amenities. The provisions made for "bubble dining domes" while homeless people's tents were violently dismantled illustrates the stark divide over who we believe should have access to public space, and what activities of living are acceptable there. On a practical level, these patio dining zones create obstacle courses for disabled people, elders, and those pushing strollers. While some cities have expanded pedestrian space by creating car-free zones, we have no guarantee that these measures will last. This is a moment when a feminist reimagining of public spaces as inclusive, caring, comfortable, sociable, and playful must be prioritized.

The hardening of cities into fearful, overpoliced, and exclusionary environments forms part of the background of the Black Lives Matter movement. The murder of George Floyd by a Minneapolis police officer in May 2020 led to months of protests—a fantastic use of public space—and calls to defund the police. For perhaps the first time, mainstream media, city politicians, and "progressives" were forced to take seriously the demands of abolitionists who are envisioning a radical overhaul of society that would make police and prisons obsolete. In *Feminist City*, I argue against a carceral feminism that locates women's safety from gendered violence in the expansion of the criminal punishment system. As I've had the opportunity to learn more about feminist perspectives on abolition from authors like Mariame Kaba and Lola Olufemi, I've become more certain that a care perspective is central to radically rethinking what safety means and what justice looks like.[6]

In a patriarchal and often violently-misogynistic society, people are rightly concerned about women's safety and their freedom from violence, harassment, and fear in urban spaces. Many ask, how will women be kept safe without police and prisons? We need to flip that question around and instead ask, has policing ever meaningfully contributed to women's safety, especially if those women aren't white, middle-class, cisgender, documented citizens? Indeed, there's no evidence that violence against women around the world has decreased, despite bloated police budgets and overflowing prisons.[7]

Police forces themselves are hotbeds of sexual harassment and assault against female members. The public isn't safe either: the murder of Sarah Everard in London in 2021, a crime for which a Metropolitan police officer was immediately arrested, was a stark reminder for many that police are sometimes perpetrators of crimes against women. Too often these victims are ignored because they are Black, Indigenous, or trans women. Police forces are also routinely excoriated for their handling of the few victims who do choose to report violence. Women who don't leave or fight back against assault aren't believed; those who do fight back face the prospect of prosecution and lengthy jail terms, as in the cases of Marissa Alexander, Bresha Meadows, and Cyntoia Brown.

In short, we can't hope to combat patriarchal violence against women by expanding one of the most violent and patriarchal institutions we have. Instead, we need to centre care by taking the enormous resources we've invested in systems of control and punishment and reinvesting in everything from child care to social housing to public transit to education to health care to social assistance to mental health and addiction services. For women specifically, robust social-support systems offer the ability to get out and stay out of abusive relationships and homes, which are of course the contexts where most women experience violence. For everyone else, creating a society where we all have our basic needs met and then some vastly reduces the circumstances that lead people to commit harmful acts. Setting up alternative systems of accountability and healing to address harm without resorting to rubrics of punishment and retribution recognizes the humanity and potential for change in all of us. As Kaba states, a feminist abolition ethic "underscores that our fates are intertwined and our liberation is interconnected."

We shouldn't have to wait for a crisis to rethink the ways things have always been done. However, if these challenging times produce a wider consensus about—or at least a willingness to consider—a set of changes that reflect that different priorities, I'm grateful. Cities have the chance to realign spaces and services to a wider set of values, including care, equity, justice, collectivity, and sustainability. Whether they do or not will depend, in part, on our (un)willingness to return to a "normal" that so profoundly harmed, disadvantaged, and exploited so many. My hope is that when you finish this book, you're more able to imagine a different way of doing cities and more ready to ask for—no, demand—a care-full feminist city for everyone.

INTRODUCTION CITY OF MEN

I have an old picture of my little brother and I surrounded by dozens of pigeons in London's Trafalgar Square. I'm guessing from our matching bowl cuts and bell-bottom corduroys that it's 1980 or 1981. We're happily tossing out seeds that our parents purchased from a little vending machine in the square. You won't find those machines anymore because feeding the pigeons is strictly frowned upon, but back then it was one of the best parts of our trip to visit my dad's family. We were in the centre of everything, our excitement palpable. In our glowing faces I see the beginning of our mutual lifelong love of London and city life.

Josh and I came into the world via downtown Toronto, but our parents raised us in the suburbs. Although Mississauga's population makes it one of the largest and most diverse cities in Canada, its essence in the 1980s was car-centred suburban mall-scape. My brother and I each moved to Toronto as soon as we could, rejecting suburbia faster than we could say "Yonge-University-Spadina Line." But our experiences of city life have been vastly different. I doubt Josh has ever had to walk home with his keys sticking out from his fist or been shoved for taking up too much space with a baby stroller. Since we share the same skin colour, religion, ability, class background, and a good chunk of our DNA, I have to conclude that gender is the difference that matters.

DISORDERLY WOMEN

Women have always been seen as a problem for the modern city. During the Industrial Revolution, European cities grew quickly and brought a chaotic mix of social classes and immigrants to the streets. The Victorian social norms of the time included strict boundaries between classes and a firm etiquette designed to protect the purity of high status white women. This etiquette was fractured by the increased urban contact between women and men, and between women and the city's great seething masses. "The gentleman and, worse still, the gentlewoman were forced to rub shoulders with the lower orders and be buffeted and pushed with little ceremony or deference," writes cultural historian Elizabeth Wilson.[1] The "contested terrain" of Victorian London had opened space for women to "claim themselves as part of a public," especially with respect to debates about safety and sexual violence, explains historian Judith Walkowitz.[2] However, this chaotic transition time meant it was increasingly difficult to discern status and a lady on the streets was at risk of the ultimate insult: being mistaken for a "public woman."

This threat to the supposedly natural distinctions of rank and the shakiness of barriers of respectability meant that for many commentators of the time, urban life itself was a threat to civilization. "The condition of women," explains Wilson, "became the touchstone for judgments on city life."[3] Women's gradually expanding freedoms were thus met with moral panic over everything from sex work to bicycles. The countryside along with the newly expanding suburbs would provide a suitable retreat for the middle and upper classes and most importantly, safety and continued respectability for women.

While some women needed to be protected from the city's messy disorder, other women were in need of control, re-education, and perhaps even banishment. Growing attention to city life made the conditions of the working class more visible and increasingly unacceptable to the middle class. Who better to blame than women, who had come to cities to find work in factories and domestic service, thus turning the family "upside down," according to Engels. Women's participation in paid labour meant some small amount of independence and of course less time for domestic responsibilities within their own homes. Poor women were cast as domestic failures whose inability to keep clean homes was to blame for the "demoralization" of the working class. This demoralization expressed itself through vice and other kinds of problematic private and public behaviours. All of this was viewed as a deeply unnatural state of affairs.

Of course, the greatest social evil was that of prostitution, which had the potential to destroy the family, shake the foundations of society, and spread disease. In the pre-germ theory understanding of the time, disease was believed to be spread by an airborne miasma carried by noxious sewer odours. The concept of a *moral* miasma emerged as well: the idea that one could be infected by depravity via sheer proximity to those who carried it. Writers of the time were scandalized by the common presence of "streetwalkers" who openly plied their trade, tempting good men into a world of vice. Women were also "constantly exposed to temptation, and, once 'fallen', a woman was doomed, many reformers believed, to a life of increasing degradation and an early and tragic death."[4]

The solution proposed by many, including Charles Dickens, was for fallen women to emigrate to the colonies where they might marry one of many surplus settler men and be restored to respectability. Out here, the need to protect white women settlers from the menace of the "native" provided one rationale for the containment and elimination of Indigenous populations from urbanizing areas. Popular novels of the day depicted sensational stories of kidnap, torture, rape, and forced marriage of white women by marauding, vengeful "savages." These new fortified settler cities would mark the transition from frontier to civilization and the purity and safety of white women would complete the metamorphosis.

On the flip side, Indigenous women were seen as threats to this urban transformation. Their bodies carried the capacity to reproduce the "savagery" that colonizers sought to contain. They also held important positions of cultural, political, and economic power in their communities. Stripping Indigenous women of this power by imposing European patriarchal family and governance systems while simultaneously dehumanizing Indigenous women as primitive and promiscuous laid the groundwork for the legal and geographic processes of dispossession and displacement.[5] Thus, the degradation and stigmatization of Indigenous women were part of the urbanization process. Given the extraordinary rates of violence against Indigenous women and girls today in settler colonial cities, it's clear that these attitudes and practices have had lasting, devastating legacies.

Fast forward to today: efforts to control women's bodies to advance certain kinds of city improvement agendas are far from over. In very recent history we've seen the forced or coerced sterilization of women of colour and Indigenous women who receive social assistance or are seen as dependent on the state in some way. The racist stereotype of the Black "welfare queen" was circulated as part of the narrative of failing cities in the 1970s and 1980s. This has been connected to moral panics over teen pregnancy with their assumptions that teen moms will join the rolls of said welfare queens and produce criminally-disposed children. Contemporary movements to abolish sex work have been re-labelled as anti-trafficking campaigns with trafficking cast as a new form of sexualized urban threat. Unfortunately, sex workers who aren't trafficked are accorded little respect or agency under this new agenda.[6] Anti-obesity campaigns target women as individuals and as mothers, with their bodies and their children's bodies viewed as symptoms of modern urban issues such as car dependency and fast food.

In short, women's bodies are still often seen as the source or sign of urban problems. Even young white women having babies have been villainized as the culprits of gentrification, while proponents of gentrification blame single mothers of colour and immigrant women for reproducing urban criminality and slowing down urban "revitalization." There seems to be no end to the ways in which women can be linked to urban social concerns.

While I concede that some of the more exaggerated Victorian's fears about purity and cleanliness have lessened, women still experience the city through a set of barriers–physical, social, economic, and symbolic–that shape their daily lives in ways that are deeply (although not only) gendered. Many of these barriers are invisible to men, because their own set of experiences means they rarely encounter them. This means that the primary decision-makers in cities, who are still mostly men, are making choices about everything from urban economic policy to housing design, school placement to bus seating, policing to snow removal with no knowledge, let alone concern for, how these decisions affect women. The city has been set up to support and facilitate the traditional gender roles of men and with men's experiences as the "norm," with little regard for how the city throws up roadblocks for women and ignores their day-to-day experience of city life. This is what I mean by the "city of men."

WHO WRITES THE CITY?

In the midst of working on this book, I was uncharacteristically excited to receive my glossy University of Toronto alumni magazine because this time the cover story was *The Cities We Need*.[7] The current president of U of T is an urban geographer, so I had high hopes. Inside were four articles about urban "needs:" affordability, accessibility, sustainability, and more fun. Great topics. But each article was written by a middle-aged white man. Most of the experts cited by the authors were men, including the ubiquitous Richard Florida, whose outsized influence on urban policy around the world through his (self-confessed) deeply-flawed creative class paradigm might in fact be to blame for many of the current affordability problems plaguing cities like Vancouver, Toronto, and San Francisco. I'd like to say I was surprised or disappointed, but resigned is probably the best word. As feminist scholar Sara Ahmed cleverly points out, "Citationality is another form of academic relationality. White men is reproduced as a *citational relational*. White men cite other white men: it is what they have always done . . . White men as a well-trodden path; the more we tread *that way* the more we go *that way*."[8] Urban scholarship and planning has been "going that way" for a good long while.

I'm far from the first feminist writer to point this out. There is, by now, a deep history of women writing about urban life (like Charlotte Brontë in *Villette*), women advocating for the needs of urban women (such as social reformers Jane Addams and Ida B. Wells), and women coming up with their own designs for homes, cities, and neighbourhoods (like Catharine Beecher and Melusina Fay Peirce). Feminist architects, urban planners, and geographers have made significant interventions in their fields through rigorous empirical research into gendered experiences. Activists have pushed hard for important changes to urban design, policing practices, and services to better meet women's needs. And yet, a woman will still cross the street at night if a stranger is walking behind her.

The foundational work of feminist urban scholars and writers before me is the backbone of the book. When I first "discovered" feminist geography in graduate school, something clicked for me. Suddenly the theoretical insights of feminist theory took on a third dimension. I understood the operation of power in a new way and fresh insights about my own experiences as a woman living in the suburbs and then the city started to pile up. I never looked back and I'm proud to call myself a feminist geographer today. Throughout this book, we'll meet the urban thinkers who have studied everything from how women travel through the city to the gendered symbolism of urban architecture to the role of women in gentrification. But rather than start with theory or policy or urban design, I want to begin from what poet Adrienne Rich calls "the geography closest in," the body and everyday life.[9]

"Begin with the material," writes Rich. "Begin with the female body.... Not to transcend this body, but to reclaim it."[10] What are we reclaiming here? We're reclaiming personal, lived experience, gut knowledges, and hard-earned truths. Rich calls it "Trying as women to see from the center," or, a politics of asking women's questions.[11] Not essentialist questions, based on some false claim to a biological definition of womanhood. Rather, questions that emerge from the everyday, embodied experience of those who include themselves in the dynamic and shifting category "women." For us, city life generates questions that for too long have gone unanswered.

As a woman, my everyday urban experiences are deeply gendered. My gender identity shapes how I move through the city, how I live my life day-to-day, and the choices available to me. My gender is more than my body, but my body is the site of my lived experience, where my identity, history, and the spaces I've lived in meet and interact and write themselves on my flesh. This is the space that I write from. It's the space where my experiences lead me to ask, "Why doesn't my stroller fit on the streetcar?" "Why do I have to walk an extra half mile home because the shortcut is too dangerous?" "Who will pick up my kid from camp if I get arrested at a G20 protest?" These aren't just personal questions. They start to get to the heart of why and how cities keep women "in their place."

I started writing this book as the "Me Too" movement exploded.[12] In the wake of investigative reporting that exposed long-time abusers and harassers in Hollywood, a wave of women and several men came forward to tell their stories about the scourge of sexual harassment and violence across workplaces, sports, politics, and education. Not since Anita Hill spoke out has the harm of sexual harassment generated such a level of media, institutional, and policy attention. While the rhetoric used to discredit survivors and whistleblowers has not changed much since the Clarence Thomas hearings, the (almost literal!) mountains of evidence against the worst culprits and most misogynist institutions are convincing many that something must change.[13]

Survivors of this abuse have testified to the long term, life-altering effects of continually facing physical and psychological violence. Their stories resonate with the vast literature on women's fear in cities. The constant, low-grade threat of violence mixed with daily harassment shapes women's urban lives in countless conscious and unconscious ways. Just as workplace harassment chases women out of positions of power and erases their contributions to science, politics, art, and culture, the spectre of urban violence limits women's choices, power, and economic opportunities. Just as industry norms are structured to permit harassment, protect abusers, and punish victims, urban environments are structured to support patriarchal family forms, gender-segregated labour markets, and traditional gender roles. And even though we like to believe society has evolved beyond the strict confines of things like gender roles, women and other marginalized groups continue to find their lives limited by the kinds of social norms that have been built into our cities.

"Me Too" survivors' stories expose the continued prevalence of what feminist activists call "rape myths:" a set of false ideas and misconceptions that sustain sexual harassment and violence in part by shifting the blame to victims. Rape myths are a key component of what we now call "rape culture." "What were you wearing?" and "why didn't you report it?" are two classic rape myth questions that "Me Too" survivors face. Rape myths also have a *geography*. This gets embedded into the mental map of safety and danger that every woman carries in her mind. "What were you doing in that neighbourhood? At that bar? Waiting alone for a bus?" "Why were you walking alone at night?" "Why did you take a shortcut?" We anticipate these questions and they shape our mental maps as much as any actual threat. These sexist myths serve to remind us that we're expected to limit our freedom to walk, work, have fun, and take up space in the city. They say: The city isn't really for you.

FREEDOM AND FEAR

A decade or so after starting that pigeon feeding frenzy, Josh and I were back in London, old enough now to take the Tube to Tottenham Court Road and Oxford Street by ourselves. Our parents probably just wanted to enjoy some kind of culturally-uplifting experience without being asked when we were going shopping every five minutes. Like the pigeons you'll now find smartly navigating the Tube to their new favourite food sources, we taught ourselves to think and feel our way through the city on our own. Long before smartphones, we just had the Tube map and our instincts to guide us. We never felt afraid. The signs and announcements about safety and vigilance conjured distant news clips of IRA bombings, but this was nothing that could touch a couple of Canadian kids on vacation. By the end of the trip, we were (in our own minds) savvy little urban explorers only a step or two removed from being real Londoners.

About a year before that trip we went to New York City for the first time. This would have been 1990, a few years before Mayor Rudy Giuliani's "zero tolerance" policies accelerated the Disney-esque makeover of Times Square and other iconic neighbourhoods. We had a little freedom to roam the big shops of Fifth Avenue together, but there was no possibility of hopping on the subway alone here. In fact, I don't think we took the subway once the whole trip, even with our parents. New York was a completely different beast than Toronto or London. For our parents, the excitement of this city was laced with a palpable sense of threat that seemed much more real than an IRA attack.

I think I learned then that a city—its dangers, thrills, culture, attraction, and more—resides in the imagination as well as in its material form. The imagined city is shaped by experience, media, art, rumour, and our own desires and fears. The gritty, dangerous New York of the 1970s and 1980s held sway in our parents' minds. It wasn't what we experienced in 1990 but it shaped what we knew or thought we knew about the place. And in fact, that hint of danger was alluring. It made New York *New York*: not Toronto, not London, and certainly not Mississauga. The energy and pull of the city was tangled up with the sense that anything might happen.

This tangled up sense of excitement and danger, freedom and fear, opportunity and threat, contours so much feminist thinking and writing about cities. As early as the 1980s, my own future PhD supervisor boldly claimed "a woman's place is in the city."[14] Gerda Wekerle was arguing that only dense, service-rich urban environments could support women's "double days" of paid and unpaid work. At the same time, sociologists and criminologists were raising the alarm over women's extremely high fear of urban crime, fear which couldn't be explained by actual levels of stranger violence against women.[15] For feminist activists, acts of public violence against women sparked the first Take Back the Night demonstrations in cities across Europe and North America as early as the mid-1970s.

In everyday life, the statements "the city is not for women" and "a woman's place is in the city" are both true. As Elizabeth Wilson attests, women have long flocked to city life despite its hostilities. She suggests that "there has perhaps been an over-emphasis on the confinement of Victorian womanhood to the private sphere," noting that even in this era of strict gender norms, some women were able to explore the city and take on new roles as public figures.[16] Dangers be damned. The city is the place where women had choices open up for them that were unheard of in small towns and rural communities. Opportunities for work. Breaking free of parochial gender norms. Avoiding heterosexual marriage and motherhood. Pursuing non-traditional careers and public office. Expressing unique identities. Taking up social and political causes. Developing new kinship networks and foregrounding friendship. Participating in arts, culture, and media. All of these options are so much more available to women in cities.

Less tangible, but no less important, are the psychic qualities of the city: anonymity, energy, spontaneity, unpredictability, and yes, even danger. In Charlotte Brontë's *Villette*, heroine Lucy Snowe travels alone to London and as she dares "the perils of crossings" she experiences "perhaps an irrational, but a real pleasure."[17] I'm not trying to say that women like being fearful, but that some of the pleasure of city life relies on its inherent *unknowability* and on one's courage in braving that unknowability. In fact, unpredictability and disorder can come to represent the "authentically urban" to women who reject safe suburban conformity and repetitive rural rhythms.[18] Of course, finding urban disorder exciting is a little easier if you have the means to retreat when you want to. In any case, fear of crime has not kept women from cities. However, it's one of many factors that shape women's urban lives in particular ways.

This book takes on women's questions about the city, looking at the good and the bad, the fun and the frightening, in order to shake up what we think we know about the cities around us. To see the social relations of the city—across gender, race, sexuality, ability, and more—with fresh eyes. To spark discussion about other, less visible kinds of urban experiences. To open space for thinking creatively about what might generate a feminist city. To bring feminist geography into conversation with the everyday nitty gritty of trying to survive and thrive, struggle and succeed, in the city.

FEMINIST GEOGRAPHY

I was on my way to one of the big annual geography conferences in Chicago in 2004 when I read that long-time anti-feminist *Globe & Mail* columnist Margaret Wente had also "discovered" feminist geography.[19] Since hating men and knowing your national capitals are clearly two totally different fields, who could believe that feminist geography was a legitimate subject? Wente used her incredulity to illustrate to her followers her regularly-recycled claim that the humanities and social sciences were worthless enterprises full of made-up disciplines and fake academics.

What the willfully ignorant Wente had no desire to understand was that geography adds a fascinating dimension to feminist analysis. Of course, you have to be willing to get beyond your middle school perception of geography: it's not about colouring in maps or memorizing continents. Geography is about the human relationship to our environment, both human-built and natural. A geographic perspective on gender offers a way of understanding how sexism functions on the ground. Women's second-class status is enforced not just through the metaphorical notion of "separate spheres," but through an actual, material geography of exclusion. Male power and privilege are upheld by keeping women's movements limited and their ability to access different spaces constrained. As feminist geographer Jane Darke says in one of my favourite quotes: "Any settlement is an inscription in space of the social relations in the society that built it.... *Our cities are patriarchy written in stone, brick, glass and concrete.*"[20]

Patriarchy written in stone. This simple statement of the fact that built environments reflect the societies that construct them might seem obvious. In a world where everything from medication to crash test dummies, bullet-proof vests to kitchen counters, smartphones to office temperatures, are designed, tested, and set to standards determined by men's bodies and needs, this shouldn't come as a surprise.[21] The director of urban design for Toronto, Lorna Day, recently found that the city's guidelines for wind effects assumed a "standard person" whose height, weight, and surface area corresponded to an adult male.[22] You'd never think that gender bias influences the height and position of skyscrapers or the development of a wind tunnel, but there you have it.

What sometimes seems even less obvious is the inverse: that once built, our cities continue to shape and influence social relations, power, inequality, and so on. Stone, brick, glass, and concrete don't have agency, do they? They aren't consciously trying to uphold the patriarchy, are they? No, but their form helps shape the range of possibilities for individuals and groups. Their form helps keep some things seeming normal and right, and others "out of place" and wrong. In short, physical places like cities *matter* when we want to think about social change.

The gendered symbolism of the urban built environment is one reminder of who built the city. Feminist architect Dolores Hayden's explosively titled 1977 article "Skyscraper Seduction, Skyscraper Rape" rips into the male power and procreative fantasies embodied by the development of ever-taller urban structures. Echoing the usual male monuments to military might, the skyscraper is a monument to male corporate economic power. Hayden argues that the office tower is one more addition "to the procession of phallic monuments in history—including poles, obelisks, spires, columns and watchtowers," as architects used the language of base, shaft, and tip and rendered upward-thrusting buildings ejaculating light into the night sky via spotlights.[23] The phallic fantasy of the skyscraper, suggests Hayden, hides the reality of the violence of capitalism, made manifest in the deaths of construction workers, bankruptcies, and the hazards of fire, terrorism, and structural collapse. As feminist geographer Liz Bondi puts it, it's not really about the symbolism of the phallus so much as its verticality is an icon of power via the "masculine character of capital."[24]

The language of architecture draws on the idea that gender is a binary opposition, with different forms and features described as masculine or feminine. Bondi suggests that these codings of the built environment "interpret gender difference as 'natural' and thereby universalize and legitimize a particular version of gender differentiation."[25] Beyond specific architectural fea-tures, gender norms are further encoded through the separation of spaces of work and home, public and private. The continued underrepresentation of women in architectural and planning professions means that women's experiences of and in these places are likely to be overlooked or based on outdated stereo-types. However, as Bondi notes, simply "adding" women to the profession or considering their experiences is inadequate on two fronts. Since women's experiences are shaped by a patriarchal society, smoothing the rough edges of that experience via urban design doesn't inherently challenge patriarchy itself. And second, assuming unity among women fails to account for other salient markers of social difference.

Historically, feminist geography—like academic feminism more widely—was concerned with "adding women" to a male-dominated discipline. The title of Janice Monk and Susan Hanson's classic intervention from 1982 speaks loudly about the field's biases: "On not excluding half of the human in human geography."[26] But the additive approach to addressing exclusion has always lacked transformative power.

In the 1970s and 1980s, Black and women of colour feminists like Angela Davis, Audre Lorde, and the women of the Combahee River Collective were challenging the mainstream women's movement to come to terms with the different forms of oppression faced by women outside the white, heterosexual middle class. Their work led to the development of what we now call intersectional feminist theory, based on the term coined by Black feminist scholar Kimberlé Crenshaw in 1989 and further developed through the 1990s by Black feminists such as Patricia Hill Collins and bell hooks.[27] Intersectionality led to a radical shift in how feminism understood the relationships among various systems of privilege and oppression including sexism, racism, classism, homophobia, and ableism.

Feminist geographers faced especially rocky terrain in a discipline steeped in a history of exploration, imperialism, and discovery. The masculine, colonial tropes of intrepid explorers mapping the "new world" still ripple through the field of geography. Urban geographers seek out the next interesting neighbourhood to study and social group to classify, while planners aspire to heights of technical, rational, and objective decision-making about how people should live in cities. Feminist urban scholars pushed to have women recognized as valid and in some ways distinct urban subjects. But their early work lacked an intersectional analysis of how gender relations interlocked with race, class, sexuality, and ability.

Retracing the trajectory taken by academic feminism across many disciplines, feminist geographers often drew on their own experiences to explore how gender interlocked with other social inequalities and the role that space played in structuring systems of oppression. The early work of Gill Valentine, for example, investigated women's fear of violence in public spaces but quickly evolved to examine lesbian experiences of everyday spaces, such as the street. Valentine faced years of professional harassment for her lesbian identity, yet work such as hers paved the way for subfields such as geographies of sexuality, lesbian geographies, and queer and trans geographies. Laura Pulido and Audrey Kobayashi drew on their experiences as women of colour in the discipline to call out geography's whiteness and push feminists to examine the implicit whiteness behind their research topics and conceptual frameworks. Today, the work of scholars like Black feminist geographer Katherine McKittrick and Indigenous feminist geographer Sarah Hunt continues to challenge lingering anti-Black and colonial attitudes that reappear in feminist and critical urban geographies through our discourses, methods, and choice of research spaces.[28]

For me, to take a feminist stance on cities is to wrestle with a set of entangled power relationships. Asking "women's questions" about the city means asking about so much more than gender. I have to ask how my desire for safety might lead to increased policing of communities of colour. I have to ask how my need for stroller access can work in solidarity with the needs of disabled people and seniors. I have to ask how my desire to "claim" urban space for women could perpetuate colonial practices and discourses that harm the efforts of Indigenous people to reclaim lands taken and colonized. Asking these kinds of questions requires an intersectional approach and some level of self-reflection on my own position.

Starting from my own body and my own experiences means starting from a pretty privileged space. As a white, cis, able-bodied woman I know that in most cases, I have the right kind of body for moving through the post-industrial, leisure, and consumption-oriented modern city. I speak English in an English-dominated country. I have formal citizenship in two nation-states. My settler status on Indigenous land is rarely questioned. I'm not Christian but being Jewish is unremarkable in Canada and not visible to most, although a resurgence of anti-Semitic rhetoric and violence makes me type that with a sense of increased wariness. In general, as someone who writes about gentrification for a living, I'm very aware that my body reads as a marker of successful "renewal," signifying that a space is respectable, safe, middle-class, and desirable.

My body might also signify danger or exclusion for people of colour, Black people, trans folks, disabled people, Indigenous people, and others for whom spaces dominated by whiteness and normative bodies are not welcoming. My presence could suggest that a petty complaint to the manager or a life-threatening phone call to the police is a moment away. My comfort will likely be prioritized over their safety by those around me and by the city in general. While I can't change most of the features that mark me in these ways, I can be aware of what my body signifies and check the impulse to assert that I can and should claim all urban spaces for my own. If my presence is going to lead to the further marginalization of already-struggling groups, then I need to strongly consider whether my presence there is necessary.

This embodied privilege doesn't negate gendered fears and exclusions in my life. Rather, the privileges that I hold intersect with and inform my experiences as a woman. Throughout the book, I try to be transparent about what my partial perspective offers, and what it obscures. Working with the commitment to understand that all knowledge is situated—i.e., all knowledge comes from some-*where*—requires me to acknowledge that even where I am (or was) an "insider," for example, in my hometown of Toronto, my perspective isn't definitive.[29] For many other cities that I write about, I'm an outsider, which means I must guard against reproducing sloppy stereotypes or problematic images of urban communities to which I don't belong. I also have to be explicit about the fact that my urban experiences and my geographic expertise are rooted in global north cities and western bodies of research. While I've sought out relevant examples and case studies from a wider range of places, I'm not able to do justice to "women's questions" arising from global south and Asian cities. This gulf is a persistent problem in feminist urban geography, one that many have identified as a key challenge for twenty-first century scholars.[30]

If you've flipped through to my author's bio, you'll have noted, maybe with some puzzlement, that I work at a small university in the territory of Mi'kma'ki in what's currently known as eastern Canada. While we have indie cafés, a hipster bar, and even a gluten-free bakery, Sackville, New Brunswick is a rural town of around five thousand people. It sits about forty kilometres from the nearest city, Moncton, whose population would easily fit inside one London borough. Not exactly an urban hotspot. The pigeons that have set up camp on my office roof are the most urban element of my day. They scribble and scrabble their way across the slanted ceiling, cooing and fighting. The university is trying to get rid of them, but obviously I root for them to avoid their executioners.

I've lived here for ten years. When I was first offered a nine-month contract, I nearly turned it down after realizing how tiny Sackville was. "I can't live there," I thought. "I'll turn it down tomorrow." That's how bound up the city was with my personal identity. After a restless night, though, I realized that as much as I loved Toronto, full-time employment wasn't to be rejected. One contract stretched into three and finally a tenure-track appointment and tenure. Ten years. Long enough that I can no longer consider it a temporary relocation from Toronto. But I remain an urban geographer and a city lover.

Where to begin? Begin with the material. The matter of the body. Adrienne Rich lists the particularities of her body—scars, pregnancies, arthritis, white skin, no rapes, no abortions—as a reminder of how her body keeps her grounded in her own perspective, of what it allows her to write and speak. What does my body allow me to write and speak? I could begin with my once-pregnant body, sweating and nauseated on a north London train. I could begin with my tired shoulders, aching from forcing a stroller through ice-choked Toronto streets. I could begin with my feet, slipping gratefully out of my hot shoes and into the cool grass of High Park, where I lie back and people watch. This meeting point of bodies and cities is at the heart of "asking women's questions" and thinking about the "feminist city."

These questions ultimately have to help us imagine and enact different urban futures. Inequality, violence, and deprivation still plague cities around the world. Dangerous nationalist movements are finding expression in acts of white terrorism that target diverse urban communities. Climate change is bringing serious challenges to questions of where and how we live. And the effects of all of these issues are very much intertwined. Although large-scale changes at both individual and societal levels are required, we needn't invent universalizing grand visions or utopian schemes in order to start making things different, better. Alternative visions already exist, both in design and in practice. From schemes to make public transportation safer for women to visions of police and prison abolition, activists, scholars, and everyday folks have long dreamed and theorized and practiced different ways of being together in cities. In fact, we all have the capacity to make new urban worlds—feminist urban worlds—even if those worlds only last a moment, or only exist in one little pocket of the city. Part of the challenge is recognizing where those alternatives are already in play and figuring out if they can be scaled up or adapted to different environments. In this book I'll share a variety of those kinds of projects, both old and new. My hope is that you can learn to see those alternatives on the ground, to have your own conversations about gender, feminism, and city life and find your own ways to take action on doing cities differently.

CHAPTER 1 **CITY OF MOMS**

If you've ever been pregnant, the "geography closest in" gets real strange, fast. Suddenly, you're someone else's environment. And everything about how your body moves through the world and is perceived by others is about to change.

I was pregnant with my daughter Maddy over a typically dreary London winter and through what felt like an unusually warm spring and summer. I had a part-time office job in Kentish Town. My commute from Finchley Central was only five Tube stops but most days it felt interminable. When I worked a morning shift, my nausea would force me off the train at Archway where I'd stumble to a bench and try to calm my stomach before gingerly re-boarding a new train. Before I was visibly pregnant there was no chance of being offered a seat, no matter how waxy and green my face. This lack of hospitality didn't improve much even after my belly expanded.

I was determined to be one of those pregnant people who carried on with their normal lives as though nothing had changed. This was long before Serena Williams won a Grand Slam tournament while pregnant but, I was channeling that kind of spirit. I was a recent women's studies graduate with my own copy of *Our Bodies, Ourselves*. I was prepared to be fierce and stick to my feminist principles in the face of the pathologizing, misogynist medical profession. I soon found that since midwives still dominated pre- and post-natal care in Britain, my anger at the system was a little misdirected. But I wasn't at all prepared for the way that my place in the city was changing.

I hadn't yet heard of "feminist geography" but I was certainly a feminist, and my feminist self was bristling at every turn. My body had suddenly turned into public property, available for touching or comment. My body was a big inconvenience to others and they didn't mind letting me know. My body's new shape had taken away my sense of anonymity and invisibility in the city. I could no longer blend in, become part of the crowd, people watch. I was the one being watched.

I didn't know how much I valued these things until they were gone. They didn't magically re-appear after my daughter was born, either. Pregnancy and motherhood made the gendered city visible to me in high definition. I'd rarely been so aware of my embodiment. Of course my gender is embodied, but it's always been there. Pregnancy was new and it made me see the city in new ways. The connection between embodiment and my experience of the city became much more visceral. While I'd experienced street harassment and fear, I had little sense of how deep, how systemic, and how geographical it all was.

THE FLÂNEUSE

As a woman, a complete sense of anonymity or invisibility in the city had never fully existed for me. The constant anticipation of harassment meant that any ability to glide along as one of the crowd was always fleeting. Nonetheless, privileges such as white skin and able-bodiedness gave me some measure of invisibility. Blending seamlessly into the urban crowd, freely traversing the streets, and engaging in detached but appreciative spectatorship have been held up as true urban ideals since the explosive growth of industrial cities. The figure of the flâneur, emerging prominently in Charles Baudelaire's writing, is a gentleman who is a "passionate spectator" of the city, seeking to "become one flesh with the crowd," at the centre of the action and yet invisible.[31] The philosopher and writer of urban life Walter Benjamin further crystallized the flâneur as an essential urban character in the modern city, and urban sociologists such as Georg Simmel located traits like a "blasé attitude" and the ability to be anonymous as inherent to the new urban psychology.[32] Not surprisingly, given the perspectives of these writers, the flâneur was always imagined as a man, not to mention one who is white and able-bodied.

Could the flâneur be female? Feminist urban writers have been divided here. Some see the model of the flâneur as an exclusionary trope to critique; others, as a figure to be reclaimed. For those who reject the idea, women can never fully escape into invisibility because their gender marks them as objects of the male gaze.[33] Others say the female flâneur has always existed. Calling her the flâneuse, these writers point to examples like Virginia Woolf. In Woolf's 1930 essay "Street Haunting: A London Adventure," the narrator imagines glimpses into strangers' minds as she walks the streets of London, musing that "to escape is the greatest of pleasures; street haunting in winter the greatest of adventures."[34] In her own diary, Woolf wrote "to walk alone in London is the greatest rest," implying that she found a measure of peace and detachment among the surging crowds.[35] Geographer Sally Munt proposed the idea of the lesbian flâneur as an urban character who sidesteps the usual pathway of the heterosexual gaze and finds pleasure in observing other women.[36]

Lauren Elkin attempts to recover the invisible history of the flâneuse in her book *Flâneuse: Women Walk the City*. Elkin argues that women have been simultaneously hyper-visible and invisible in the streets. Always watched, yet written out of accounts of urban life. She describes her own youthful experiences of *flânerie* on the streets of Paris, long before she knew it had a name: "I could walk for hours in Paris and never 'get' anywhere, looking at the way the city was put together, glimpsing its unofficial history here and there. . . . I was on the lookout for residue, for texture, for accidents and encounters and unexpected openings."[37] Elkin insists the reluctance of men like Baudelaire, Benjamin, and Simmel to imagine a female flâneur comes from their inability to notice women acting in ways that didn't fit their preconceived notions. Women walking in public were more likely to be read as streetwalkers (sex workers) than as women out for another purpose. But Elkin writes, "If we tunnel back, we find there always was a flâneuse passing Baudelaire in the street."[38]

I have to wonder though, is the flâneuse ever pregnant or pushing a stroller? Artist and scholar Katerie Gladdys' video "Stroller Flâneur" plays on the word stroller (a synonym for flâneur) as it depicts her pushing a baby stroller through her Gainesville, Florida neighbourhood. As the mommy flâneuse, she searches for "patterns and narratives in the genealogies of architectural structures and topographies while simultaneously searching for items of interest for [her] son." Gladdys claims that "the performance of strolling a child is indeed one of the social processes of inhabiting and appropriating the public spaces" of the city. While I agree, and I would argue that moms pushing strollers are invisible in their own way, they're not usually associated with the classic figure of the flâneur.[39]

And even the reclaimed flâneuse still inhabits a "normal" body, one able to move in unremarkable ways through the streets. None of the writers who talk about *flâneuserie* give mention to the pregnant body. While not all those who experience pregnancy are women (e.g. trans men), it's certainly a state rife with gendered assumptions. If it was already a stretch to imagine the female version of the flâneur, then the idea of a pregnant flâneur is likely beyond the pale.

A PUBLIC BODY

It's impossible to blend in when your body has suddenly become public property. Although women often experience comments on our bodies and uninvited physical contact, pregnancy and motherhood elevate these intrusions to a new level. People read my protruding belly as if it said, "rub here please!" I was expected to cheerfully welcome all manner of unsolicited advice and to express appropriate amounts of shame and remorse for any lapse in following the reams of often contradictory "expert" tips on eating, drinking, vitamins, exercise, work, etc. I was no longer an individual making my own choices. It was like they'd been crowdsourced without my consent.

All of this made me extraordinarily aware of my body, and not in a good way. If the urbanite's blasé attitude toward others is what allows each of us to maintain some sense of privacy in the crowd, its loss made me feel very public. I was embarrassed by my belly's showy-ness, tackily thrusting my intimate biology into the civilized public sphere. I didn't want to glow. I wanted to hide. I wasn't trying to disguise my pregnancy, but I was overcome with an urge to modesty that no amount of feminist body positivity could shake. My friends loved to tease me about the number of crop tops in my wardrobe, but I could never bring myself to wear a shirt that exposed my belly even a little while pregnant. Was I trying to put a barrier between myself and the many strangers who felt comfortable commenting on or touching my body? Was it part of my perplexing embarrassment over being such an obviously biological animal? Had I unknowingly embraced the Cartesian mind-body split for so long that my body's sudden assertiveness made me doubt everything I knew about myself?

Perhaps ironically, strangers' fascination with my body didn't translate into much of an uptick in urban courtesy. In fact, I sensed a constant, low-grade reminder that I was now different, Other, and out of place. This was most obvious to me on the Tube, where I was rarely offered a seat during my rush hour commute. Posh businessmen deliberately buried their faces in the broadsheets, pretending not to see me. One time I relinquished my seat to an even more pregnant woman before anyone took notice of either of us. Anna Quindlen tells an identical story about being pregnant in New York, offering her seat to a woman who "looked like she should have been on her way to the hospital." "I love New York," Quindlen writes, "but it's a tough place to be pregnant.... There's no privacy in New York; everyone is right up against everyone else and they all feel compelled to say what they think."[40] People who have been pregnant share these sorts of stories with a wry chuckle, like old war stories, as if they're rights of passage when you're pregnant in the city. As if it's all to be expected for daring to leave your home with your messy, inconvenient body.

My efforts to reclaim the spirit of the flâneuse resumed after Maddy was born. Maddy would sleep for ages if she was strapped into a baby carrier, snug against my chest. I'd plot a route to a newly opened Starbucks with my trusted London A-Z map book and head out for a simple treat: a latté and fresh scenery. These breaks in the exhausting routine of feeding, rocking, bathing, and so on felt like a tiny bit of freedom. I almost remembered what it was to be a young person in the city before having a baby.

Sometimes these outings went well, sometimes not. My attempts to be the mommy flâneuse were continually interrupted by the messy biology of a newborn. Places that used to feel welcoming and comfortable now made me feel like an outsider, an alien with leaking breasts and a loud, smelly baby. It's hard to play the detached observer when the fleshy, embodied acts of parenthood are on full display. I wanted to be indifferent about it all, believe me. While Maddy snoozed away I could almost pretend that I wasn't seconds away from a wet disaster. When she woke, hungry or dirty, I scuttled off to the public washroom to ensure that no one had to bear witness to the natural realities of parenting.

I'd never realized how gutsy it was to do things like breast-feed in public. I knew intellectually that I was "allowed" to nurse my baby anywhere, but the thought made me cringe. The weird mix of reactions to my body that I'd experienced while pregnant taught me that I could never predict how I'd be made to feel. It was jarring to be revered and resented in equal measure. I was a divine figure in need of protection, but also out of place and taking up space in ways that make other people uncomfortable. The fact that news items about people being asked to leave public places while breastfeeding pop up on a regular basis—with breastfeeding explicitly protected by human rights laws in Canada—suggests that strong convictions about the proper place of breastfeeding parents remain in place.

When behaving correctly, keeping my inconvenient body contained, and parenting my baby in ways that satisfied dozens of strangers at once, I received smiles and assistance. The instant my presence became too big, too noisy, too embodied, I met angry glares, snide comments, and sometimes even physical aggression. There was the man who kept shoving me forward while in line at the grocery store. When I asked him to stop he told me to "get my damn stroller out of the way." There was the woman on the incredibly crowded bus who called me a bad mother because Maddy accidentally stepped on her foot. There was the sales clerk in a Toronto department store who actually told me to wait while she finished serving a customer when I rushed up to the desk because Maddy had toddled off out of sight. Obviously she was found, but only thanks to another mom who rushed into action when she heard the panic in my voice.

This level of rudeness didn't happen every day, but underlying all of this social hostility was the fact that the city itself, its very form and function, was set up to make my life shockingly difficult. I was accustomed to being aware of my environment in terms of safety, which had a lot more to do with *who* was in the environment, rather than the environment itself. Now, however, the city was out to get me. Barriers that my able-bodied, youthful self had never encountered were suddenly slamming into me at every turn. The freedom that the city had once represented seemed like a distant memory.

A WOMAN'S PLACE

As I tried to navigate an unfamiliar set of everyday routines as a new mom, the city was a physical force I had to constantly struggle against. Wasn't the city supposed to be the place where women could best juggle the demands of their double and triple days of social reproduction, paid work, school, and myriad other roles? Didn't my PhD supervisor proclaim that a "woman's place is in the city"?[41] If that was true, why did every day feel like a fight against an enemy that was invisible yet all around me?

It's true that I could walk to the grocery store, café, parks, and many other places I needed to access. I could take transit to school and the nearest subway stop was within walking distance. There were community centres and schools with programs for small children. Maddy's day care was reasonably nearby. I could function without a car. Compared to the suburbs, this kind of urban density offered a lot more ways to manage parenting, grad school, and domestic responsibilities. In fact, what Gerda Wekerle (my supervisor) was responding to when she wrote "a woman's place is in the city" in the 1980s was the nightmare of suburban living.

There is of course a long history of feminist critiques of the suburbs. Betty Friedan's 1963 diagnosis of the "problem that has no name" included a scathing indictment of suburban life:

Each suburban wife struggles with it alone. As she made the beds, shopped for groceries, matched slipcover material, ate peanut butter sandwiches with her children, chauffeured Cub Scouts and Brownies, lay beside her husband at night, she was afraid to ask even of herself the silent question—'Is this all?'[42]

From *The Stepford Wives* to *Desperate Housewives*, *Weeds* to *Mad Men*, suburban life has generated endless stereotypes. The Valium-popping housewife, the overprotective mom, the housewife with a dark secret, etc. And there's no small amount of things to critique in terms of lifestyle, gender roles, and racial and class inequality. But feminist geographers were also looking at the very material of the suburbs, their form, design, and architecture as foundational sources of the "problem that has no name."

We take the suburbs largely for granted now as a kind of organic outgrowth of big cities and a result of a natural need for more space and bigger family homes. However, the suburbs are anything but natural. Suburban development fulfilled very specific social and economic agendas. From providing much-needed housing for returning soldiers and their growing families to giving a boost to the post-war manufacturing sector, the suburbs were an essential component of a plan to sustain economic growth, especially after World War II. In North America, government programs facilitating home ownership turned us into nations of home owners, tying workers to their mortgages in a move that some felt would produce a more conservative, and importantly, anti-communist society. The residential real estate sector grew into one of the most significant components of the twentieth-century economy—so significant, that when the U.S. housing sector was undermined by risky lending practices in 2007, it triggered a global economic crisis. Perhaps most critically, as feminist architect Dolores Hayden notes, "single family suburban homes have become inseparable from the [North] American dream, of economic success and upward mobility. Their presence pervades every aspect of economic, social, and political life."[43]

The economic role of suburban development was essential, but there was a social agenda as well, one that would massively affect race and gender relations. In the U.S., the post-WWII suburban boom coincided with a period when millions of African Americans were leaving the rural south in search of better opportunities in the industrial cities of the north. Rapid increases in the Black population of these cities tested the tolerant attitudes of the "progressive" north. Many white households preferred to decamp to the suburbs in a phenomenon that became known as white flight. Indeed, many early mass-produced suburbs such as the famous Levittowns were explicitly "whites only." Over the long term, this pattern meant that non-white communities were confined to the crumbling, underfunded, and over-policed inner city and denied opportunities for wealth accumulation via home ownership. This is a major factor in continuing urban patterns of racial segregation and wealth disparity well into the twenty-first century.[44]

If the racial effects of suburban development linger today, so too do the gendered effects. Hayden puts it succinctly: "Developers argued that a particular kind of house would help the veteran change from an aggressive air ace to a commuting salesman who mowed the lawn. That house would also help a woman change from Rosie the Riveter to a stay-at-home mom."[45] Post-war propaganda was explicit about the need for women to relinquish their wartime factory jobs to returning men and the suburban home was the perfect "fix" for re-establishing normative gender roles. By providing a spatial solution to the temporary widening of women's horizons, the public-private, paid-unpaid work divide could be "naturally" re-established between the sexes.

The suburban lifestyle both assumed and required, in order to function properly, a heterosexual nuclear family with one adult working outside the home and one inside. Large houses, isolated from transit and other services, meant the stay-at-home wife and mother was required to perform a full-time domestic caretaker role, overseeing the home and managing the needs of the breadwinner and children. As feminist planner Sherilyn MacGregor states, this built form has "created a lasting infrastructure for the [gendered] division of labour," one that pre-supposes the traditional heterosexual nuclear family.[46]

Hayden contends that only a small fraction of households includes the sole male breadwinner/unemployed housewife with minor children. Indeed, this model has likely always been a small proportion of households and it rarely represented the lives of Black and working class women. And yet the predominant residential landscape is designed with this ideal. Because the built environment is durable over long time spans, we're stuck with spaces that reflect outdated and inaccurate social realities. This, in turn, shapes how people live their lives and the range of choices and possibilities that are open to them.

During one of my not-infrequent rants about this, a friend accused me of giving the suburbs "too much agency" in this example. So let me clarify: the suburbs are not consciously *trying* to keep women in the kitchen and out of the workplace, but given the assumptions they rest upon, the suburbs will actively (if not agentically) stymie attempts to manage different family shapes and working lives. The isolation, size of the family home, need for multiple vehicles, and demands of child care can continue to push women either out of the workplace or into lower-paying, part-time jobs that mostly allow them to juggle the responsibilities of suburban life. It's rarely the male breadwinner's career that is sacrificed or downsized. After all, given the long-standing gender pay gap, it makes no sense to limit the man's earning potential. In this way, the suburbs continue to support and naturalize certain kinds of gender roles in the heterosexual family and in the labour market.

THE CITY FIX

Gerda Wekerle and many others argued that relative to the suburbs, cities offered much better prospects for women working outside the home who needed to juggle multiple conflicting roles. For families headed by women, "their very survival," argues Wekerle, is dependent "on a wide network of social services frequently found only in central city areas."[47] Research in the 1970s and 1980s found women use the city more intensively than men, are "more involved in work, neighbourhood and cultural activities than suburban women and most of these opportunities are lost when they move to the suburbs."[48] In the early 1960s, famed urban planning critic Jane Jacobs challenged the prevailing idea that the suburbs were good places for women and children. She noted isolation, a lack of people on the streets, and car dependency as concerns that particularly affected women while also contributing to the decline of the public realm in general.[49]

The city, however, isn't a magic fix for these concerns. Leaving aside the question of whether making it easier for women to take on disproportionate household burdens is the end goal, cities still contain multiple barriers. Cities are based around the same kinds of assumed social norms and institutions as the suburbs. Geographer Kim England writes that gender roles are "fossilized into the concrete appearance of space. Hence the location of residential areas, work-places, transportation networks, and the overall layout of cities in general reflect a patriarchal capitalist society's expectations of what types of activities take place where, when and by whom."[50] All forms of urban planning draw on a cluster of assumptions about the "typical" urban citizen: their daily travel plans, needs, desires, and values. Shockingly, this citizen is a man. A breadwinning husband and father, able-bodied, heterosexual, white, and cis-gender. This has meant that even though cities have a lot of advantages relative to the suburbs, they're certainly not built with the aim of making women's "double shifts" of paid and unpaid work easier to manage.

We can see this in the way that public transit has been set up, particularly since the rise of suburbia. Most urban public transportation systems are designed to accommodate the typical rush hour commute of a nine-to-five office worker. What little transit that does exist in the suburbs is designed to carry this commuter in a specific direction at a specific time. The whole system assumes a linear trip without detours or multiple stops. And this has worked pretty well for the usual male commuter.

However, research shows that women's commutes are often more complex, reflecting the layered and sometimes conflicting duties of paid and unpaid work.[51] A mother with two small children uses the local bus to drop off one child at day care when it opens at eight, then doubles back on her journey to leave the other child at school at eight-thirty. She gets on the train, rushing to work for nine. On the way home the journey is reversed, with an extra stop to pick up missing ingredients for dinner and a pack of diapers. Now laden with packages, a stroller, and a child, she fights her way back onto the crowded bus to finally head home. Many transit systems will force her to pay multiple times for this trip and for the children, too. If she lives in the suburbs, she might even have to pay to access different municipal systems. Recent research has found that transportation is yet another area where women pay a "pink tax" (paying more for similar services than men). Women are more likely to rely on public transportation than men, although they're more poorly served by it. Sarah Kaufman's research showed that in New York City for example, women who are primary caregivers for children may be paying up to seventy-six dollars extra per month on transportation costs.[52]

When I became a mum, I quickly realized that using public transit with a baby stroller in London was a joke. Although a lot of Tube stations have elevators because the stations are so deep underground, only fifty out of two hundred and seventy stations are accessible.[53] Curved staircases, random steps, steep escalators, sharp turns, narrow tunnels, and of course thousands of commuters and tourists make navigating the system an adventure. One of our first big outings with newborn Maddy was to a baby show (like a home show, but with baby stuff). We had a big comfy pram, of the kind still common in the U.K. and Europe, that we'd found at a charity shop. It might as well have been a spaceship, that's how out of place it was on our journey. That was the first and last time we used the pram. We learned that the only accessible way to navigate the city with a baby was with her in a carrier.

Once back in Toronto, Maddy was rapidly getting too big for the carrier. There was no way to avoid taking the stroller on the TTC. At the time, none of my local stations had elevators or even down escalators. Every time I wanted to go down the steps, I had to stand at the top and wait for someone to offer help. We'd awkwardly and somewhat unsafely lug the stroller, taking up way too much space and slowing everyone down. Once Maddy was big enough, I moved her into the most compact stroller possible, one light enough to hoist onto my hip. It wasn't ideal, but better than the time a man insisted on helping me and ended up falling backwards down the steps. Luckily, he released his end of the stroller before he bumped down a dozen steps on his rear end. I was mortified, although he was ultimately unhurt. Young mother Malaysia Goodson wasn't so lucky. She died after stumbling on the steps of a New York City subway station while carrying her daughter in a stroller. Although her death wasn't a direct result of the fall, this dangerous moment highlights a "nightmare scenario" that parents risk everyday on inaccessible and crowded public transit systems.[54]

Architect and new mother Christine Murray asks "What would cities look like if they were designed by mothers?"[55] Transit issues loom large in her discussion, as she recalls crying when her nearest Tube station was revamped without an elevator. She also laments the lack of space on buses for wheelchairs, connecting lack of accessibility for mothers to issues facing seniors and disabled people. Every aspect of public transit reminded me that I wasn't the ideal imagined user. Stairs, revolving doors, turnstiles, no space for strollers, broken elevators and escalators, rude comments, glares: all of these told me that the city wasn't designed with parents and children in mind. I sheepishly realized that until I faced these barriers, I'd rarely considered the experiences of disabled people or seniors who are even more poorly accommodated. It's almost as though we're all presumed to want or need no access to work, public space, or city services. Best to remain in our homes and institutions, where we belong.

The idea that the design, funding, and scheduling of mass transit systems are gender equality issues has seen little traction, despite transit being a major area of women's urban activism. In 1976, women in the northern city of Whitehorse developed the Yukon's first mass transit system (four minibuses) as a response to the lack of access to good paid employment that women faced in the cold, sprawling city.[56] In 2019, young women from a slum resettlement colony in South Delhi recorded a rap song about their urban lives, tackling one of their biggest concerns: "the absence of a safe and affordable commute."[57] Mostly, those who run mass transit systems have shown a willful ignorance about women's needs. When a pregnant commuter traveling to and from work in London in 2014 was forced to sit on the floor when passengers refused her a seat despite her direct request, she complained to the rail company. They suggested that if she felt unwell she could pull the emergency cord or simply avoid travel during rush hour.[58]

GENTRIFYING MOTHERHOOD

When we moved back to Toronto, high rents pushed me further out of the central city than I would have liked, but at least I had some access to shopping and services in my neighbourhood, right? True, but what I started to glean was that these conveniences stemmed partly from the fact that my neighbourhood was in the early stages of gentrification. Gentrification is basically the process whereby working class, lower income neighbourhoods get taken over by middle-class households and businesses. There are a lot of causes and forms of gentrification, but my neighbourhood—the Junction—was experiencing a kind of start-stop slow motion transition when I first moved there in early 2000. My local "amenities" included a Blockbuster Video and a No Frills grocery store. There were a few playgrounds but at least one was often filled with trash and needles. Still, I could walk to the main commercial strip for most of our basic needs, and things weren't yet too expensive.

Early feminist writing on gentrification noted that a "back to the city" movement for middle-class families works like a geographic fix for the problems women face juggling work and home.[59] As women entered the higher-paying professional workforce in ever-greater numbers, postponed the age of marriage and child-bearing, and even opted out of the heterosexual family altogether, they sought urban environments that could accommodate their needs and provide the necessary services. As feminist geographer Winifred Curran puts it, "women were not only potential beneficiaries of gentrification, but drivers of the process" as well.[60] Theorists predicted that given these gendered trends in the workforce, family, and housing, major shifts in the land use patterns of cities would surely follow. However, no fundamental changes have occurred that actually alter the city in ways that serve women's equality. Indeed, we could argue that many changes, including widespread gentrification, have made urban environments less resourceful for the majority of women.

Gentrifying neighbourhoods attract amenities that serve middle-class parents: clean parks, cafés, bookstores, places to buy fresh and wholesome food, etc. They're often located near good transit routes and centred around good schools, especially in the U.K. and U.S. According to Curran,

> Gentrification offered a market-oriented, individualized, privatized spatial solution to the problem of work-life balance. With urban planning failing to catch up to the lived experiences of urban dwellers, those who could afford to found more advantageous spaces in which to attempt the balance, "rediscovering" inner city neighbourhoods which offered easy access to downtown jobs and other amenities.[61]

But Curran goes on to note that even the class-based advantages brought by gentrification don't fundamentally disrupt either the gendered division of domestic labour or the urban infrastructure designed to accommodate the movement and work patterns of men. She argues, and I agree: "the narrative of urban living for the affluent tends to minimize, or ignore altogether, the role of care and family in urban design."[62] The lack of play spaces, preschools, and sometimes even grocery stores in proximity to new urban housing developments such as condominiums suggests that planners and policy-makers are still not interested in providing workable/liveable spaces for families, even those who can afford to live in these shiny new urban habitats.[63]

Care work is still very much an afterthought in cities, and gentrification doesn't suddenly make things easier, especially for the majority of women for whom the "amenities" of gentrification are out of reach. In my experience those amenities are a bit of a double-edged sword when coupled with the social trend that some have called the "gentrification of parenting." This concept builds on the idea of "intensive mothering," a term coined by sociologist Sharon Hays that she defines as "child centred, expert guided, emotionally absorbing, labour intensive, and financially expensive."[64] These accelerated expectations around the amount of dedicated, undivided attention parents are supposed to provide are unprecedented. As maternal scholars like Andrea O'Reilly argue, intensive mothering and a new "mystique of motherhood" emerged just in time to add fuel to the fiery backlash toward women's increased social, sexual, and economic independence in the 1970s and 1980s.[65]

This intensification manifests in a variety of conspicuous consumption practices and aesthetics that some have called the "gentrification of parenting." The norms and cultural signifiers of good parenting have been gentrified as they're increasingly defined by the particular product brands, styles, and kinds of activities purchased and practiced by middle and upper class urban households. This plays out in the urban environment as middle-class parents demand and draw resources to their neighbourhoods and provide a market for upscale shopping and carefully curated child-centred activities.[66] The amount of time, money, and emotional labour required to do this parenting work is simply not available to most families and mothers in particular.

Reminiscing about those early years of parenting in my gentrifying neighbourhood doesn't evoke a sense of ease. In fact, it evokes a deep bodily sense of exhaustion. Sure, lack of sleep is typical for new parents. What I'm referring to is the physical exertion of intensive parenting in the city. I picture my younger self, pushing a plastic-wheeled stroller across sidewalks and streets choked with snow and ice. Loading the stroller full of groceries several times a week because we didn't have a car. Note: this is supposed to be one of the "convenient" parts of city living. Half-carrying, half-dragging that stroller home because a wheel would disintegrate after taking a battering on pocked pavements. Multiple daily trips to the park, a literacy drop-in, or a community centre play space to fulfill my daughter's "need" for enriching, sociable, exciting activities. Evening transit trips to swimming lessons downtown. The constant back and forth of day care, school, errands, lessons, visits to family and friends. I want to go back in time and tell myself: stay home. Lie down. Do less.

Doing less didn't seem like an option at the time, although many of the stay-at-home moms in my neighbourhood were stunned to learn I was taking a full graduate school course load. What they didn't know was that school was the easiest part of my day. Being in my head for a few hours, without being immediately responsible for the tiniest demands of another human *and* worrying about her mental and emotional growth ... it was so peaceful. Even the archetypal suburban mom of the 1950s wasn't expected to constantly entertain her children. But the supposedly emancipated urban mom of the late twentieth and early twenty-first centuries must fulfill a complex set of domestic responsibilities alongside all of this child enrichment, usually while working outside the home as well. And she does it in spaces most decidedly not set up to support her labour.

I used to think that Maddy's city childhood—and my urban parenting—was much different from the suburban childhood I had in the 1980s. It seemed like she had a lot more fun activities oriented to her interests and a lot less sitting in the car waiting for parents to finish their errands. That part is probably true, but certainly intensive parenting was already on the rise in the 1980s. I remember weekends filled with synagogue, dance lessons, baseball practices, swimming, skating, and Hebrew school as well as chores and schlepping across Mississauga on a seemingly endless series of domestic errands. My parents were doing their best to manage the demands of home, work, and parenting in an increasingly sprawling landscape with one car and only one driver's license between them.

Before she learned to drive, my mom would often walk forty-five minutes or an hour just to run a simple errand. Maybe she just wanted an excuse to get out of the house, a little time to herself in the shops without grumpy children in tow. Looking back, I see that we were performing pretty similar juggling acts as moms. Although living in the city meant that I had better access to transit and services, it was hardly a magic solution to the multiple demands on my time.

More affluent families manage these contradictions by relying on others' low-waged labour. Immigrants, women, and men of colour perform the outsourced work of social reproduction when families can't manage on their own or when the state refuses to help (for example, by providing affordable child care). As a graduate student with a partner working in a low-paying blue-collar industry, I didn't have much to spare for paid services. Even so, when the time and energy demands of all that juggling wore me down, we justified going deeper into credit card debt for extras like grocery delivery and transit passes. Paying for Maddy's various activities wasn't all about enrichment; these activities functioned as childcare so I could steal thirty minutes to do schoolwork in the pool gallery. My own enrichment—completing higher education—relied in part on the availability of the underpaid labour of others (delivery people, child care workers), driving home for me how the lack of public infrastructure for care work deepens inequality among women as we participate in multiple layers of exploitation in order to keep ourselves afloat.

This imbalance has global implications, reshaping the lives of mothers in cities around the world. As the demand for help with domestic care labour rises among wealthier working women, transnational women migrants have been conscripted to fill this care labour deficit. In Singapore, domestic workers from the Philippines and Indonesia allow Singaporean women to participate in the city-state's drive to become a world-leading financial and communications-centred global city. Feminist geographers Brenda Yeoh, Shirlena Huang, and Katie Willis note that, as in many other cities, Singaporean women who work outside the home have been unsuccessful in transferring a sufficient share of domestic and childcare responsibilities to men, compelling them to rely, often reluctantly, on foreign domestic maids.[67]

In Canada, thousands of women—mostly mothers themselves—from places like the Philippines and the Caribbean come to Canada as temporary migrants to work as nannies, housekeepers, and home care workers. Feminist geographer Geraldine Pratt's long-term research with Filipina migrants in cities like Vancouver has highlighted stories of loss and disconnection, as mothers leave their children behind—sometimes for decades—to care for children in Canada. Back home, their children are raised by husbands, grandparents, relatives, or neighbours in a patchwork of care arrangements that sow a heartbreaking emotional distance that might never be overcome. Pratt describes the ways in which the former lives of Filipina migrants are made invisible to us here in Canada, with separation from their husbands and children just a "shadowy existence" that our reliance on their labour forces us to forget.[68]

When my marriage ended, the demands only intensified. The nights Maddy spent at her dad's place weren't especially restful. Drop-offs and pick-ups meant more bus trips with the added stress of betting on the timing of an unreliable system to avoid irritating the other parent. Extra tasks and expenses now included journeys to lawyers and counselors, courts, and social workers. I struggled to figure out how I could possibly be everywhere I had to be while coordinating Maddy's care and supervision. I was writing my dissertation and teaching classes at three different universities, adding expensive trips on the Greyhound bus and commuter trains to my already inefficient daily travel patterns.

There were times when Maddy had to be left alone for short periods or walk herself halfway to school before meeting a friend. The gaps in the fabric of our household were constantly expanding. Looking back, I don't really know how I managed it all without disaster striking. Certainly, my privileges as an educated, white, cisgender woman helped to keep us all afloat, but I wasn't immune to increased surveillance from the state in the form of social workers who demanded that Maddy be provided with certain services. They of course didn't provide those services. That fell to me. I learned firsthand how the state shifts burdens to mothers and how poorly my neighbourhood and city supported me.

The really annoying thing is that there was nothing unusual about my situation. The traditional nuclear family is no longer the norm. Cities are full of blended families, complex kinship relations entailed by divorce and remarriage, lone parents, queer relationships, polyamorous families, foster families, migration of family members, non-family households, multi-generation households, empty nesters, and more. But you wouldn't know it by looking at the way our cities and their suburbs are designed to function.

Ideally, all of these diverse kinship networks could open up possibilities for sharing the work of social reproduction, caregiving, and child-raising in creative, even feminist, ways. For that to happen, however, our neighbourhoods and cities have to support it. The massive construction of small one or two-bedroom condominium units in high rise apartment buildings has left a shortage of affordable housing for families. Clogged roads and expensive transit systems make it difficult to get kids to and from the homes of extended kin, and then on to school, daycare, and activities. A lack of secure, full-time employment for many parents means juggling the demands of precarious work and perhaps being forced to leave a convenient neighbourhood to find suitable work. Gentrification pushes out single parents, low-income people, and affordable services, scattering kin across the city.

THE NON-SEXIST CITY
Although the full diversity of family and household forms may be somewhat new, ideas for creating housing developments and even whole neighbourhoods that collectivize and facilitate care work can be found as recently as the 1980s and 1990s and as far back as the late 1800s in North America. Hayden's book *The Grand Domestic Revolution: A History of Feminist Designs for American Homes, Neighborhoods, and Cities* detailed the utopian schemes and sometimes actual homes and communities designed by early materialist feminists who argued that housework and childcare must be socialized and incorporated into new spatial arrangements to facilitate women's entry into the workforce, equality with men, and intellectual development.[69]

Visions of the "non-sexist city" often centre housing issues, noting that the nuclear family home is a really inefficient way to utilize labour, one that keeps women tied to the home with little time or energy for other pursuits.[70] Housing developments that allow households to share the work of cooking, cleaning, and caring for children are common features of feminist designs. Wekerle notes that in the 1970s and 1980s, before federal funding for subsidized housing was scaled back in the first wave of neoliberalism, a variety of cooperative housing developments that focused on lower-income groups with specific needs—single mothers, older women, disabled women—were built in cities across Canada.[71] These examples can remind of us that there are already existing alternatives. Some of the work of imagining the non-sexist city has already been done.

When I started my master's degree with a child under one year of age and no way to afford day care (wait lists for subsidized spots were outrageous), I scrambled to find time to complete my work. Luckily, I met Anneke. We had classes together and discovered that we were both the primary caregivers for very young kids. I started bringing Maddy to Anneke's house two days a week and we took turns watching the kids while one of us left for a few hours to study. The little bit of extra time afforded by what I liked to call the "city's smallest babysitting co-op" made a huge difference. At the time, I thought that we were just lucky. I didn't realize that we were part of a long tradition of mothers and other caregivers coming up with ingenious arrangements for doing care work in the city. These creative practices of "getting by" have informed feminist urban interventions since the nineteenth century.

Yet, many decades after trenchant critiques of how cities and suburbs fail mothers and other caregivers, the same problems remain. Under neoliberalism, most of the "solutions" generated for those problems have been market-based, meaning they require the ability to pay for extra services, conveniences, and someone else's underpaid labour. Very few changes, especially in North American cities, have re-imagined and re-worked the built environment and other aspects of urban infrastructure in ways that take care work seriously.[72]

In Europe, "gender-mainstreaming" approaches to urban planning and budgetary decisions have a longer history. Essentially, these frameworks mean that every planning, policy, and budget decision has to be considered with the goal of gender equality as the departure point. For example, policymakers must ask how a decision will potentially enhance or undermine gender equality. These approaches push cities to consider how decisions support or stymie the care work that literally keeps society functioning.

The city of Vienna has adopted a gender mainstreaming approach in several areas, such as education and health care. But it has had a profound affect on urban planning.[73] Echoing the experiences of women around the world, and my own experiences too, women responded to a 1999 transit survey with their stories of complex journeys balancing care and paid work: "I take my kids to the doctor some mornings, then bring them to school before I go to work. Later, I help my mother buy groceries and bring my kids home on the metro."[74] Transit use illustrated some of the vast discrepancies between men's and women's use of city services and spaces. Vienna attempted to meet this challenge by redesigning areas to facilitate pedestrian mobility and accessibility as well as improving public transport services. The city also created housing developments of the sort imagined by feminist designers, including on-site childcare, health services, and access to transit. With the objective of making sure that everyone has equal access to urban resources, Vienna's gender mainstreaming approach is "literally reshaping the city."

Taking a gender-centred perspective on planning doesn't have to be limited to wealthy global north cities. Women in informal settlements in global south mega-cities are also working to reclaim urban planning. Faced with critical challenges such as poverty, lack of secure tenure, poor sanitation, and few sexual and repro-ductive health services, women have often banded together to form collectives that help them improve economic opportunities and advocate for security of housing and tenure. For example, the Shack Dwellers Federation of Namibia is a collective offering "shared security of tenure and housing to their members, thereby improving women's opportunities to get better public services and generate income."[75] Prabha Khosla identifies "gender-sensitive slum upgrading" as an area of action, noting that women must be included as decision-makers to ensure access to affordable land, with close proximity to work and essential services.

Gender mainstreaming is slowly making its way into more cities. Recently, news media seemed amused to report that some Canadian and U.S. cities were using a gender analysis on their snowplow budgets and schedules.[76] While it's fair to say that snow doesn't discriminate, decisions about which roads and areas to prioritize for clearance reveals a lot about which activities are valued in the city. In most cases, cities plow major roads leading to the central city first, leaving residential streets, sidewalks, and school zones until last. In contrast, cities like Stockholm have adopted a "gender equal plowing strategy" that instead prioritizes sidewalks, bike paths, bus lanes, and day care zones in recognition of the fact that women, children, and seniors are more likely to walk, bike, or use mass transit. Moreover, since kids need to be dropped off before work begins, it makes sense to clear these routes earlier. The vice mayor of Stockholm, Daniel Helldén, described the plan to Canadian media, arguing that instead of plowing in ways that reinforce car-centred behavior, Stockholm's method encourages everyone to use alternative modes of transportation. Instead of replicating the status quo, their plan looks forward to "how you want your city to be."[77]

Gender mainstreaming has its limitations. City officials in Vienna note there's a danger of reinforcing already existing gender norms and roles around paid and unpaid work, for example.[78] For example, in Seoul, efforts to make working women's commutes easier—with everything from "high heel friendly" pavements to "pink" parking spots designated for women—have not been matched by state efforts to balance inequities in domestic and childcare labour.[79] Taking gender as the primary category for equality can also be limiting. While the typical urban citizen has too often been narrowly imagined as a white, cis, able-bodied, middle class, heterosexual man, the imagined female citizen of gender planning has been similarly limited. A married, able-bodied mother with a pink- or white-collar job has usually been the imagined beneficiary of gender-sensitive planning. This woman is increasingly likely to represent a minority in most contemporary cities, suggesting that there are large groups of women whose needs may be unmet by gender mainstreaming.

Travelling outside of the central city illustrates these disparities and their spatial components. When I started my PhD, my commute up to York University on the Keele Street bus took me through low-income, racialized neighbourhoods where even more outrageous demands on mothers became apparent. Although still technically urban, these are neighbourhoods where walking to a full-service grocery store is rarely an option. Taking public transit means waiting unsheltered in the freezing cold or blazing sun for inaccessible, unpredictable buses. Fulfilling daily needs means making multiple stops at different shops and strip malls. The prospect of these moms finding thirty minutes to read the paper in a Starbucks during the baby's nap seemed highly unlikely.

Geographer Brenda Parker writes compellingly about the experiences of low-income African American women in Milwaukee.[80] Parker argues that gentrification and cutbacks to urban social services result in "amplification" and "intensification" effects on the everyday lives and labours of these women, effects that get written on the body in the form of exhaustion, illness, and chronic pain. Navigating the city isn't just tiring in terms of negotiating treacherous stairs and overcrowded transit. These inconveniences are layered with the time- and energy-sucking work of navigating both "state and 'shadow' provisioning options, such as travelling to food pantries and churches; meeting with social workers, teachers, and food stamp offices; and the endless waiting at agencies and health clinics."[81]

Combined with over extended, poorly paid workdays, this labour meant that even the basic responsibilities and joys of parenthood fell out of reach. One of Parker's interviewees, "Audra," shared her experience: "Because you're spending fourteen hours a day on an eight-hour a day job. So when you get home you're too tired to help them with their homework."[82] These struggles are only exacerbated by gentrification. Low-income racialized women are more vulnerable to displacement, getting pushed into under-serviced areas where the benefits of urban living—interconnected access to places of employment, schools, services, retail, transit, and home life—are decidedly thinned out.

These areas may also be zones where air pollution and issues such as contaminated water further affect the work of mothering.

Urban environmental geographer Julie Sze writes about the high rates of respiratory illness among children of colour in poor neighbourhoods, where mothers are centrally responsible for the intensive work of asthma management.[83] The struggle to provide clean water for drinking, cleaning, and bathing in the context of the Flint water crisis is another example, not to mention the work of caring for children affected by lead poisoning. As the work of motherhood becomes costlier via the gentrification of parenting, those who can afford privatized services benefit while those who cannot are shoved into neighbourhoods that make their lives even harder.

In Milwaukee, the racially-divided geography of the city also affected mothers' abilities to find good work close to home. Research with mothers in Johannesburg found that the legacies of apartheid and its lingering geographies of segregation continued to shape the choices mothers make with respect to home, work, and school in the city. For example, great disparities in the quality of schools, reflecting raced and classed geographies, meant that many mothers had to consider uprooting in order to move within the catchment range of a good school, even if that meant losing out on employment opportunities and family support. Dangerous public transport systems also meant that mothers were reluctant to send their children alone, meaning that they had to juggle work and home alongside school travel.[84]

Confronted with a dearth of support from city policy and infrastructure for their lives, low-income women are forced to find ways to weave care and paid labour together. In Parker's Milwaukee research, women "took their babies with them while they drove the bus for work; ... not uncommonly, two or three families lived together in a one- or two-bedroom apartment. There, women watched each other's children while one person 'provisioned' the household through paid labor."[85] In Johannesburg, women sometimes made the heartbreaking decision to have their children live with relatives because the limited range of choice in places to live and work hampered their ability to give their children access to amenities or good schools. These kinds of strategies have long been described by Black feminist writers like bell hooks and Patricia Hill Collins, who contend that Black women's social reproductive work has mostly been subject to punitive measures by the state, such as having children taken away or being subject to "workfare" policies.[86] Feminist activism around domestic labour has typically centred the white, heterosexual married woman and ignored the particular needs and concerns of women of colour.

While it can be dangerous to romanticize the survival strategies of low-income people of colour, their tactics and resistance strategies push feminists to think beyond gender mainstreaming. In *Urban Black Women and the Politics of Resistance*,[87] Zenzele Isoke explores how Black women resist and rework the meanings of urban space and urban politics in what she calls a "despised" city: Newark. Facing long-term disinvestment in their communities and high levels of state violence, Black women in Newark, argues Isoke, use practices of "homemaking" in the city to reconfigure a "hostile and deeply racialized landscape."[88] Here, homemaking means "creating homeplaces to affirm African American life, history, culture, and politics. Homeplaces are political spaces that black women create to express care for each other and their communities, and to remember, revise, and revive scripts of black political resistance."[89] An urban politics of care is enacted not only through an attachment to place, but as "an active and *collective working toward* physical, symbolic, and relational transformations."[90]

As a state-centred, "single issue" strategy, gender main-streaming can only take us so far. And let's face it, relying heavily on the state for radical transformation is a waste of time, and perhaps even dangerous for Black and Indigenous people and people of colour who have been deemed expendable or positioned as "problems" to be solved or disposed of in the "progressive" city. Isoke's study illustrates the power of forging alliances across diverse communities to combat racism, sexism, and homophobia to "confront and transform [the] structural intersectionality" of oppressions in the city.[91] I want cities to enact policies and create spaces that make care work and social reproduction more collective, less exhausting, and more equitable. However, I know we have to look for deeper change and more expansive and liberatory imaginings of the city in the spaces and communities that are already practicing ways of caring that bust the binaries of paid and unpaid work, public and private spaces, production and social reproduction.

Pregnancy and parenting as a woman in the city awoke my feminist urban consciousness. While experiences such as sexual harassment on city streets weren't new to me, the tightly tangled workings of social and spatial forms of exclusion—the ways the built environment and social relations collide and intermingle—were suddenly tangible. The limits on the kinds of urban subjectivities I could inhabit were crystal clear. The boundaries of anonymity, invisibility, and belonging were stark. The effects of overt forms of gendered embodiment on my day-to-day life were pressing. In this context, motherhood for me was a catalyst, one that operated through anger, frustration, disappointment, and occasionally joy, for wanting to imagine feminist urban futures.

What would care-full urban futures look like? Futures that were based around the needs, demands, and desires of women of colour, disabled women, queer women, single women care-givers, aging women, Indigenous women, and especially those for whom these identities intersect? It's clear that the time has come to decentre the heterosexual, nuclear family in everything from housing design to transportation strategies, neighbourhood planning to urban zoning. This means that city planners and architects can't take the white, able-bodied cis man as the default subject and imagine everyone else as a variation on the norm. Instead, the margins must become the centre. Although the lives of an aging widow in the inner suburbs and low-income lesbian moms renting in a gentrifying neighbourhood will look different, interventions to improve access to city services and amenities for one will likely benefit the other. Accessible transportation, plowed sidewalks, affordable housing, safe and clean public bath-rooms, access to a community garden, a liveable minimum wage, and shared spaces for things like meal preparation would relieve burdens on many kinds of households, not to mention contribute to other important goals such as environmental sustainability.

A feminist city must be one where barriers—physical and social—are dismantled, where all bodies are welcome and accom-modated. A feminist city must be care-centred, not because women should remain largely responsible for care work, but because the city has the potential to spread care work more evenly. A feminist city must look to the creative tools that women have always used to support one another and find ways to build that support into the very fabric of the urban world.

CHAPTER 2 **CITY OF FRIENDS**

When *Sex and the City* premiered in 1998, it was the first mainstream, big budget television show to portray both women's friendships and women's urban lives. The idea that the city of New York was actually the "fifth friend" quickly became a cliché, but it was clear viewers understood that the setting was more than a backdrop. New York's culture, energy, danger, excitement, cost, opportunities, and disappointments explicitly shape the romances, careers, families, and friendships of Carrie, Miranda, Samantha, and Charlotte. At times, city life strains their bonds of friendship. When Miranda moves to Brooklyn from Manhattan to accommodate her expanding family, she's convinced she'll never see her friends again. At other times, the challenges of the city present opportunities to support one another. When Carrie's rental apartment goes co-op, she can't afford the down payment. Recently separated, Charlotte gives Carrie her Tiffany engagement ring so that Carrie can stay in the home she loves. Although these four friends and their privileged lifestyles don't represent most women in cities, their fictional and sometimes fantastical storylines nonetheless made possible a cultural moment where female friendships were centred in a set of tales about the "struggles" of the modern urban woman.

The power of female friendship is typically either underestimated, undermined, or ignored all together in cultural narratives. There are few examples that speak to the importance of women's friendships in relation to life in the city. For all its faults, *Sex and the City* never strayed too far from its central conceit: that friendship was the life raft keeping each character afloat when other aspects of their lives threatened to drag them under. For far more ordinary women, friendships are also part of our urban survival toolkits. Although female friendship is often overlooked in favour of a focus on romantic partnerships, it's a powerful force that women rely on in multiple ways. Friendships with other women also shape the ways that women engage with the city itself.

FRIENDSHIP AS A WAY OF LIFE

In *Notes from a Feminist Killjoy*, literature scholar Erin Wunker explores female friendships as sustaining and transformational. She asks a provocative question: "What would female friendship as *a way of life* look like?"[92] Work highlighting the complexity of female friendship is much rarer than movies, television shows, and books that gloss over women's friendships to focus instead on romantic relationships, family lives, and dramatic life events. Friendship is relegated to the background as a simple plot or character device for moving the real action along. Wunker wonders what might be possible if we resist "representations of female friendships that police those friendships into invisibility or strip them of their radical potential?"[93] I wonder, what ways of being in the city are lost or ignored when we view female friendships as frivolous and disposable?

The phrase "female friendship as a way of life" resonates with me so deeply. Although my adult life has involved a strong commitment to my career, raising a child, marriage, divorce, and various romantic attachments as well as moving to another province, my friendships with other women have been the stable, consistent core and sometimes even the highest priority amongst a range of competing demands. My two main "girl gangs" have made me who I am and I couldn't imagine giving them up. One of them has endured for the better part of twenty-five years now, longer than any relationship and pre-dating parenthood and career. When I picture retirement, it's their faces I see around me. Wunker herself reflects on the constellation of support, knowledge, care, and loving critique she's received from her friendships and describes friendships among women as "world-making." In queer theory, world-making includes creative, disruptive, utopian, and even failed performances, practices, relationships, and imaginings that not only challenge structures like hetero- and homonormativity, public and private, etc., but that map queer, insurgent, *other* worlds beyond the already charted pathways.[94] World-making means the process of both imagining and creating space(s) where things can unfold *otherwise*. Practicing female friendship as a way of life is, I think, a world-making activity.

Too often, women's friendships are misunderstood as second-rate substitutions for romantic heterosexual relationships or veiled lesbian love. Certainly, there's a long, often hidden history of women's friendships as masks for actual lesbian relationships that couldn't be publicly acknowledged. Even when lesbianism isn't the subtext, close female friendships might be viewed as substitutes for romantic partnership or as supplying something that romantic partners (especially male romantic partners) cannot. Wunker worries that "recycling one storyline—the romance—means dragging all the sedimented associations of that storyline with you."[95] It seems that culturally we lack a language to adequately describe the character and quality of female friendships without resorting to borrowed vocabulary or miscategorizations.

Even more problematically, popular representations swing between the stereotype of the bitchy, jealous, always-on-the-verge-of-a-catfight friendship and the overly-mythologized, fraught, mysterious, and unknowable friendship. Wunker describes the latter as creating a "dense, atmospheric pressure surrounding discourses of female friendship."[96] In her bestselling essay collection *Bad Feminist*, Roxane Gay implores readers to "abandon the cultural myth that all female friendships must be bitchy, toxic or competitive. This myth is like heels and purses—pretty but designed to SLOW women down."[97] Gay lays down thirteen rules for female friendships, designed to tear down the damaging myths that put walls between us and constantly undermine our attempts at connection. As she notes in rule number one, these myths are designed to slow women down: they keep us locked in competition, holding one another at arm's length out of fear, jealousy, or insecurity. They keep us from joining forces and realizing the power of friendship for transforming our worlds and ourselves.

At first glance, Italian writer Elena Ferrante's acclaimed Neapolitan novels detailing decades of complicated friendship between the narrator Lenù and her neighbour Lila may seem to perpetuate the myth of the mysterious and fraught world of female friendship. However, their story is rich with moments where the girls (and eventually, women) use their friendship as a world-making force. This force allows them to challenge the confines of lives that seem bound by traditional gendered expectations as well as poverty and a complex political climate. In *My Brilliant Friend,* the first of the four novels, the young friends strike out for the sea from their dreary, working class Naples neighbourhood. The road is long but the narrator, Lenù, is undaunted:

> When I think of the pleasure of being free, I think of the start of that day, of coming out of the tunnel and finding ourselves on a road that went straight as far as the eye could see ... if you got to the end you arrived at the sea. I felt joyfully open to the unknown. . . . We walked for a long time between crumbling walls invaded by low weeds, low structures from which came voices in dialect, sometimes a clamor. . . . We held each other by the hand, we walked side by side.[98]

Braving the strange in search of new experiences, yearning to taste the sea air and glimpse a world beyond what Ferrante only ever refers to as "the neighbourhood," two girls lie to their parents and head unprepared into the unknown. Lila and Lenù's naiveté and reliance on one another remind me of many moments where my friends and I defied our parents' edicts and rushed headlong into our own urban adventures.

When we were fifteen my friend Sally and I snuck downtown for a midnight screening of *The Rocky Horror Picture Show* at what was then the Bloor Cinema. My parents were out of town and I was supposed to be spending the night at Sally's. At some point during the raucous live show that accompanied the movie, we lost what remained of our money, and therefore, our passage home to the suburbs. After some searching on the sticky theatre floors once the lights came up, we realized we were out of luck and emerged into the chilly, 2 a.m. spring air of Toronto. Confident that the city would somehow provide for us, we decided to make our way to Yonge Street. We figured that the two dollars or so left in Sally's pocket would get us a hot chocolate and a place to sit in a 24-hour coffee shop. In the morning, we'd walk down to Union Station and sneak onto a commuter train, where we could take our chances that no ticket collectors would come by. Although we were annoyed we'd lost our money, our attitude was very matter-of-fact. Together, we didn't have anything to fear.

The details are fuzzy almost thirty years later, but I don't think we made it to Yonge Street as directly as we'd hoped. We hitched a ride in the wrong direction before striking up a conversation with a couple of teenage boys who lived in the city, also under an apparent lack of parental supervision. As a group of four, we spent the rest of our night wandering up and down Yonge Street, sitting in CoffeeTime and McDonald's and sneaking into office buildings where we could lurk in the stairwells. A homeless artist drew our portraits in a coffee shop; we interrupted a fight between a couple on their way out of a club; we visited our favourite concert venue—the Masonic Temple—and sat in a parkette talking about our favourite bands. In the morning, our new friends bought us subway tokens and, seemingly out of a sense of obligation more than actual interest, asked for our phone numbers before waving us off on a westbound train.

Afterwards, the whole night felt like a dream, a tall tale no one but Sally and I would believe. Of course we couldn't tell our parents or siblings, and rapidly, the whole weird night became our secret. We spoke of it so rarely that after Sally and I passed out of each other's lives after high school, I hardly thought of it. When it came back to me I had to wonder if I imagined the whole thing. But I still have the hasty portrait that we bought from the homeless artist, sketched in black pen on the back of a McDonald's placemat, taped into my journal of the time.

Back in a fictionalized Naples, Lila and Lenù's quest doesn't ultimately take them to the sea. When the girls reach the neighbourhood boundary, things change. They enter a "landscape of ruin," filled with garbage and indifferent strangers. The sky darkens, and with a crack of thunder, opens. At Lila's behest they flee back home. Lenù's parents have been worried; they beat her. Lenù begins to wonder if Lila meant for the expedition to fail all along (friendship is complicated, remember?). At any rate, their ambitious adventure doesn't work out as planned. But Lenù's sense that with Lila at her side, her horizons were infinitely wider than she had previously imagined, persisted.[99]

Sally and I managed to hide the full truth from our parents, although I was berated for what my parents believed was a more mundane lie about where we'd held our sleepover. Neither the scolding nor the ridiculousness of the night itself deterred us from future transgressions. I know that as a sensible adult, I'm supposed to look back and say, "That was ridiculous! What were we thinking? It's a miracle we weren't murdered!" Instead I can't help but see it as a moment when our young friendship allowed us to experience the city in a whole new way, to test our own limits, and to gain a sense that the city could be a place for us. These moments of taking charge in our lives were possible because we never questioned that we could count on each other. We knew no one would be left behind or tattled on. Friendship made freedom in the city a possibility for us. In turn, the city streets intensified our bond. It wasn't just that we rebelled and broke the rules. Taking up space in the city at night—using urban public spaces at times when girls are typically excluded based on social norms and sexist limitations on mobility—was a formative, perhaps even transformative, experience.

GIRLS TOWN

Our night on the town isn't the kind of teen girl story you're likely to see in a movie or television show. In her study of major teen films from the 1980s and 1990s, feminist geographer Alison Bain found that films reproduce "the notion that girls' culture doesn't extend beyond the bedroom."[100] In these popular films, including *Fast Times at Ridgemont High, Clueless, Sixteen Candles,* and *Heathers,* among others, girls' bedrooms are the primary sites for scenes of friendship and interaction among girls, although the semi-private school bathroom also figures regularly. In public spaces, especially urban spaces, girls are portrayed as boys' "appendages" while out on dates or at public events. Urban spaces were often totally absent. Bain found "little cinematic coverage of intersections or street corners as gathering points for girls," except in films like *Foxfire* where girls' rebellion against male violence and social control is the movie's explicit theme.[101] The city doesn't seem to be a place where mainstream filmmakers imagine teen girls interacting with one another, building relationships, and claiming space.

Perhaps not surprisingly, these films showed little racial or class diversity within the teens' social groups, always centring white characters. Racial invisibility may hint at where we imagine diversity to exist: not in the private spaces of the home or the affluent suburbs. Movies that centre Black and Latina girls and their friendships are more likely to be set in cities, such as 2016's *The Fits* (Cincinnati) or 2000's *Our Song* (Brooklyn). The girls in *Our Song* struggle with everyday urban issues facing girls of colour: the closure of their high school due to asbestos, living with the threat of violent crime, and the lack of affordable health care. They try to stay connected to each other through their marching band, but face the possibility of a future where their circumstances will drive them apart.

Outside of the movies, the needs and wants of girls and young women are almost completely ignored in architecture and planning. When communities advocate for "spaces for youth," the kinds of spaces they come up with are skate parks, basketball courts, and hockey arenas. In other words, spaces that have boys in mind as users, and where girls have trouble finding access, acceptance, and safety. When Swedish architecture firm White Arkitekter actually approached teenage girls to design scale models of public space, the girls came up with "places for sitting together face to face, protected from weather and wind, to see without necessary [sic] being seen, a sense of intimacy without being constrictive; and most of all, to be able to leave an imprint on their city."[102]

Despite the lack of attention to their needs, girls *do* use urban spaces, and in a variety of creative ways. Geographer Mary Thomas studies how girls use public space in cities, querying how they resist, and also reproduce, gendered norms through their patterns of "hanging out" in various consumption spaces.[103] Subject to more spatial control than boys, girls struggle to find places to hang. They must develop their own strategies for avoiding adult surveillance and gaining permission to explore, including using the power of friendship to assuage parental fears about girls alone. Girls can even work together to make direct claims on the city. For example, girls in Hanoi formed a collective to create 'zines to educate bus drivers and passengers about girls' safety from harassment on public transit. In Kampala, a youth collective fought to improve hygiene in the city as well as more walkable infrastructure to make sure girls could continue to go to school or work.[104]

Literally smashing the idea that girls don't actively take and mark urban space was the 1996 film *Girls Town*, directed by *Our Song*'s Jim McKay.[105] Perhaps ironically, I saw the movie alone, but I walked out ready to find my girls and bust the patriarchy with a baseball bat. The slogan on the poster read: "This ain't no 90210." Far from the privileged and sensational teen lives depicted on the popular 1990s show *Beverley Hills 90210*, the girls of *Girls Town* struggled with abusive families, violent boys, poverty, teen parenthood, and a seemingly bleak future. The *Girls Town* cast was much more racially diverse than 90210's and the characters lived working class lives in an unspecified inner city neighbourhood bearing zero resemblance to Rodeo Drive. The deliberate distinction drawn by contrasting *Girls Town* and 90210 also speaks to their vastly different portrayals of female friendships.

While there are exceptions, the friendships on 90210 often fall into the tropes of jealous, catty, snobby, and mean. Enemies as often as they were allies, characters like Brenda and Kelly were in constant competition for boys, popularity, and status. *Girls Town* was different, and at the time it blew my mind to see young women portrayed as fiercely loyal to one another. Starring Lily Taylor, Bruklin Harris, and Anna Grace as high school seniors in a declining rust belt city, the movie follows three girls reeling in the wake of their friend Nikki's suicide. In trying to come to grips with the suicide, they discover Nikki had been raped. As the groups processes this new fact, Emma (played by Grace) reveals that she was recently sexually assaulted on a date. Stirred by anger and grief, the friends pledge to enact revenge on the men who have wronged them. They also support one another as they struggle with the challenges of daily life and their efforts to make it out of what seem like dead-end circumstances.

The girls first claim space by painting a mural in Nikki's memory. Graffiti is often associated with young urban men, but here the young women take a piece of the city and create a memorial, refusing to forget the sexual assault that drove Nikki to suicide. Making the mural doesn't assuage their anger, however. Lurking in one of their usual hangouts, the baseball dugout (another typically male-dominated space), Emma's friends Patti (Taylor) and Angela (Harris) decide that Emma's rapist—a fellow high school student—cannot simply slip back into his life of school and sports with no consequences. They destroy his car and tag it with the word "rapist" in the school parking lot. Finally, the friends decide they must confront Nikki's rapist, an older man from work. A smug and uncaring character, the girls must make him understand what he did to their friend.

In contrast to my other favourite teen movies such as *Pretty in Pink*, *Girls Town* didn't offer a redemptive romance or salvation from tough circumstances. For me it captured a sense of simmering rage and validated my need to be seen and heard in an indifferent and often hostile city. The movie also confirmed that the fierce female friendships I was forming in university were going to be essential for expressing these feelings.

Back in the suburbs, though, before I met the women who would become my own *Girls Town* girl gang, my friends and I struggled to find spaces to express ourselves. We wanted freedoms that our parents weren't yet willing to grant, but the spaces where we'd hung out as kids and pre-teens—bedrooms, basements, and bathrooms—were too boring, too confining, too cut off from the real world. Girls must learn to make do with the limited spaces that they're offered. In my suburban adolescence, that space was the mall.

Easily accessed, inviting no probing questions from our parents, always warm and safe. I can't begin to count the hours spent wandering the convoluted corridors of ever-expanding shopping centres in Mississauga. I suppose we were lucky that given Mississauga's size and growth rate, we had choices. Bain's study, not surprisingly, found the mall featured heavily as a setting in teen films.[106] Despite the mall's inherent homogeneity, we entertained ourselves by looking at things we couldn't afford, imagining the kind of cool people we'd be if only we had the right clothes and shoes. We found ways to make our own spaces, in stairwells, corners, and service corridors. My best friend Erika and I didn't go to the same school, so the mall was the place where we could actually be together instead of talking on the phone. But as we got older, the mall didn't reflect our changing identities. We needed to find the spaces and styles and people that would let us start to define ourselves as more than Jewish girls from the suburbs.

If the mall was our default space—easy to access, parents happy to leave us there for a few hours—then downtown, as we called neighbouring Toronto, was our aspiration. We could take a commuter train and in about thirty minutes, we'd be at the foot of Yonge Street, one of Toronto's central shopping and tourist districts. While we might venture into the enormous Eaton Centre mall, our targets were the vintage shops, used record stores, poster shops, and head shops of Yonge and Queen Streets. In the early 1990s, Yonge and Queen didn't resemble any of our familiar suburban landscapes. Pre-gentrification, thrift stores and army surplus shops reigned. Punk kids hung out on steps, glaring attractively at the shoppers. We coveted the Doc Martens we couldn't yet afford and rummaged for ripped jeans and men's shirts that would make our mothers scowl. We bummed cigarettes that we didn't actually smoke off strangers and tried to act like we belonged on these dirty sidewalks instead of under the fluorescent lights of the mall.

Of course this all feels like a cliché now. We weren't unique. Suburban girls all over seek out ways to push back against the pressures of conformity. Like most young people we were trying to figure ourselves out and "different" spaces helped us to create fresh moments for self-expression. Gill Valentine's research on adult versus youth spaces found that girls paradoxically identify public spaces, such as city streets, as "private," because these spaces allow them anonymity away from the prying gaze of parents, teachers, and other caregivers.[107] The home was strangely more like a public space, since girls didn't feel a sense of privacy or control over their bedrooms and possessions here.

As a teenager, the paradoxical privacy of downtown Toronto permitted my friends and I to explore identities frowned upon or forbidden at home. Venturing into the city, where we were unlikely to be seen by anyone we knew, meant that we could be weird or goth or simply angry for a while. But we always needed the presence and support of our friends to do it. Toronto never seemed scary to me, but the courage to go new places, wear different clothes, and speak to strange people could only come with the encouragement of girlfriends. Your friend would help you practice your new persona, forged in the incense-soaked thrift shops of Kensington Market, and then hide your less parent-friendly purchases in her basement until you could sneak them on in the school bathroom on Monday morning. Devoted female friendship mixed with the electricity of the then-still somewhat gritty city was the potent cocktail that let us grow out of suburban girlhood and into the young independent women we wanted so badly to become.

Like *Girls Town*, the 1996 movie *Foxfire* portrays high-school aged girls collectively resisting patriarchal violence and challenging limitations across gender, race, class, and sexuality. Both movies also show girls at home in the city, not as appendages to boys but as people "participating in the street life around them."[108] In *Foxfire*, "the girls wander the streets of Portland laughing, talking, drinking, smoking, and taking photographs as they explore the deserted back alleys and less travelled paths."[109] As in *Girls Town*, the girl gang in *Foxfire* comes together to confront abusive men. Inspired by the rebellious loner Legs (the very charismatic Angelina Jolie), the girls beat up a teacher and crash the car of boys who threatened to rape protagonist Maddie (played by Hedy Burress). In the final scene, Maddie climbs the girders of a bridge high over the river, one she'd been too afraid to scale before. Her transformative friendship with Legs and the other girls inspires Maddie to face her fears and accomplish the feat. Arms spread wide, Maddie stands tall above the city beneath her.

The ways that teenage girls and their friends take up space tends to be the subject of more derision than celebration. Their tastes and passionate interests are ridiculed as frivolous, childish, and uncultured. Their takeovers of mall food courts, group trips to the bathroom, and constant slumber parties are portrayed as equal parts annoying and mysterious. In a culture that routinely mocks teen girls and their interests, desires, and hobbies, there are few sources from which to imagine or recognize the ways that girls collectively shape, transform, and re-make their worlds, especially urban worlds. Bain's look at teen films showed that "unaccompanied young women are rarely depicted as transforming, commandeering or occupying space."[110] Bain thus laments that "the opportunity for the transformation of space by teenage girls to be about empowerment and about transgressive actions to claim and control space in an adult world remains underexplored."[111]

In *Girls Town* and *Foxfire*, the girls' commitment to "female friendship as a way of life" plays out in the city streets where they gradually gain more confidence, power, and control in a male-dominated, threatening environment with the shadow of sexual violence always present. Girls coming together in urban spaces challenges perceptions about who the city is for. In appropriating abandoned or masculine spaces, leaving their mark through graffiti, and occasionally, erupting into violence of their own, the city as "patriarchy in glass and stone" is re-cast as a space of possibility.[112] Girls' presence on city streets, a place where they have been deemed out of place, can and should be considered part of girls' repertoire of resistance to varied modes of control within an adult-dominated, patriarchal society.

FRIENDSHIPS AND FREEDOM

Those movies epitomized the kind of badass female friendships I wanted to find and cultivate. When I moved to the city at eighteen to attend University of Toronto, many of my high school friendships began to fade away. Luckily, I immediately met Jill, my assigned roommate in the co-ed dorm, and Kate, who had the room next door. Once Jill and I figured out that the uber-cool Kate was actually just another freshman newly transplanted from the suburbs, we became a tight trio. Although we'd all lived near Toronto most of our lives, our developing friendship led us into different spaces and new ways of exploring the city.

We reveled in the lack of direct parental oversight and the newfound freedom to make our own plans, explore new places, and enjoy the city's nightlife. We hung out in smoky coffee shops with doors off alleyways, dragging our class readings along but mostly spending the hours getting to know everything about one another. Iconic clubs like Lee's Palace, Sneaky Dees, and Sanctuary that I'd only heard about on the radio were now part of our regular weekend itinerary. For once, nothing was off limits.

That didn't mean there was never any fear. Indeed, the tension between the city as a space of liberation and the city as a space of danger loomed large. This tension had a huge influence on the ways our friendship grew and solidified. As young women who were barely adults, we brought along truckloads of absorbed parental and societal messages about strangers, urban spaces, and proverbial "dark alleys." Although these messages were deeply internalized, I discovered they had performative aspects as well. Our actual levels of fear weren't particularly relevant. Rather, we habitually *performed* acts of safety and precaution in line with our gendered socialization.

Long before anyone had cell phones, we had to concoct various little routines ensuring no one was left to walk alone at night. For example, if I was taking the subway home, I was supposed to call Jill from the pay phone when I got off at St. George Station, wait while she and Kate walked up together and then the three of us—invulnerable now—would walk back to residence. If I forgot, worry abounded. Promises were made to remember for next time.

Developing these little check-in tactics was automatic, an assumed and completely normalized part of being a woman. In her recent book *Text Me When You Get Home: The Evolution and Triumph of Modern Female Friendship*, Kayleen Schaefer writes about the work that the phrase "text me when you get home" does in female friendships:

My best friend, Ruthie, who lives a few blocks from me in Brooklyn, and I say it to each other after these kinds of nights. "I love you," one of us will say. "Text me when you get home," the other will say. We're saying the same thing. . . . Men do not tell their friends to text them when they get home.[113]

Schaefer explains that this isn't strictly about safety. It's our way of showing solidarity with one another, of mutually recognizing the gamut of risks and annoyances that any woman travelling alone is likely to face. That reminder to text, knowing that your friends will be watching their phones, or that they'll muster a posse to come and get you from the club or the subway station is an act of forging a web of connection. Schaefer writes that this web is "a way for women to tell each other, *I'm always with you. I won't forget about you when you walk away.*" Even years later, when Jill and I would meet up for drinks and then head home in separate directions, we'd stand directly across from one another on the subway platform, keeping our eyes on each other for as long as possible before a train roared into the station.

Back in university, I bristled at these unwieldy arrangements of calling, waiting, walking, etc. I knew there was minimal risk in most of our activities, even while alone. I can't remember if I already knew that women are at much greater risk from private, intimate violence than public, stranger violence, but I think I instinctively understood that dark alleys weren't harbouring dozens of rapists. And as college students, we were much more likely to face assault in our dorm than on a city street.

All the same, I don't blame us for being protective of one another. The long-feared "Scarborough Rapist" had just been apprehended in 1993, the year before we started university. His

and his wife's heinous crimes and subsequent graphic and horri-
fying trials were constant news items until at least late 1995.[114]
We had a very real sense of responsibility for one another, even
though we'd only been friends a short while. In contrast, the
men in our residence seemed determined to kill one another off
with their ridiculous masculinity contests, pouring alcohol down
one another's throats until someone ended up in the hospital or
fighting strangers on the street. Our duty to take care of one
another was clear and undeniable, no matter how exasperating
our check ins sometimes seemed.

I was grateful to have friends who cared. After every night
out we managed to get each other home, even if it meant begging
taxi drivers to accept leftover loose change. We fought off harassers in nightclubs with well-placed elbows and boots. We welcomed
each other back with tea and cookies after tense visits with family
in the suburbs. We took each other to the hospital after falls, bike
crashes, and stomach bugs. We kept each other safe, and even
more, helped each other learn to take up space, to fight back, to
be ourselves despite the constant reminders about how we were
supposed to look or behave. My friends were my safety net, my
city survival toolkit. Schaefer exclaims that her friends "are like
a life raft I didn't know I was looking for before I got on it."[115] Being
with my friends helped me to challenge the deeply-ingrained,
unconscious belief I should take up very little room, physically,
emotionally, verbally. They helped me direct my frustrations onto
schools, systems, and structures rather than other women, and
to feel strong and less afraid. Female friendship, in short, was
more than a life raft: it was power.

The emotions associated with that time in my life come
flooding back whenever I watch *Broad City*, created by real life
friends Abbi Jacobsen and Ilana Glazer. On the show, Abbi and

Ilana live in New York and are underemployed, precariously housed, and always on the verge of a personal, romantic, professional, or financial disaster. They love New York but struggle to thrive in the uncaring, expensive, frenetic city. The city spaces they inhabit, claim, resist, flee from, and sometimes fall into are part of their shared story. As a reviewer for *The Guardian* observes, Abbi and Ilana "scrounge together an existence in New York City. They work jobs they hate, have sex with guys they just aren't that into and generally make the city their playground."[116] Always in danger of injuring themselves on that playground, literally and figuratively, the two women are unfailingly supportive of one another. They are each other's urban safety net.

Broad City is a millennial version of an important story about women's lives in the city, one that's been told through iconic shows like *The Mary Tyler Moore Show*, *Kate and Ally*, *Laverne and Shirley*, and *Cagney and Lacey*. All shows that were hailed for their breakthrough representations of women, these programs had both the city as the key site for women's independence and growth, and abiding friendships as the foundational relationships that allowed the women to break out of traditional roles. Today, *Insecure*, created by and starring Issa Rae, uses Los Angeles as the setting for a story about the necessity of Black women's friendships to their survival in a world that wants to thwart their ambitions and refuses to see them as whole, complicated people. Issa and her best friend Molly (played by Yvonne Orji) struggle together through the intertwined maze of racism and sexism at work, the difficulties of finding romantic partners that respect their intellect and talent, and the challenge of keeping their girl gang together through major life changes. In contrast to the over-the-top antics of *Broad City*, *Insecure* shines a sometimes painfully realistic light on heartbreak, economic anxiety, and lack of fulfillment in the global city. Both shows, however, keep friendship (however fraught it might be) central to their characters' survival.

In turn, the city lets female friendship unfold on its own terms. In *Broad City*'s vibrant, loud, and often surreal New York, the city is sometimes like a living entity that swallows their every effort to gain stability and success. Nonetheless, it always provides a landscape for Abbi and Ilana to come together. Their "ride-or-die" commitment to each other saturates every episode. Even though they find themselves in absurd situations, often of their own making, they're always there to bail one another out without judgment. As another reviewer in *The Guardian* exclaims,

> They are buffeted about by fate more than poor Ulysses, sent from one corner of New York City to the next on a series of misadventures and brushes with death. In the first episode of the third season alone they drop their keys in a storm drain, are attacked by a passing subway car, get trapped in a porta-potty, hijacked on the back of a delivery truck, and beset by a writhing horde of rabid customers at a pop-up shop.[117]

But every scrape they find their way out of seems designed to give the viewer another window into the depth of their friendship. *Broad City* doesn't entertain any of the negative stereotypes about women's friendship, not for a minute. Instead, we get to see female friendship as committed, lifelong, and badass.

Erin Wunker suggests that prioritizing female friendship, even writing about it or representing it on the screen, is an act of insurgency that starts to unmake the tightly woven cloth of heteronormativity, capitalism, reproductive labour, and domesticity.[118]

Together, Abbi and Ilana, Issa and Molly, repeatedly and decisively and sometimes very messily fail to meet the norms and standards of adulthood and heterosexual relationships. But in that failure, they generate a world—and a city—where their friendship can be the axis around which everything else turns.

The city itself can help women's friendships thrive. Women make friends in the suburbs, sure. But the design of the suburban landscape encourages a private, inward focus. Moving from garage to suv with no need to go outside, burdened with the care of a large home, encouraged to make use of the backyard as a private recreational space: the suburban woman may have few opportunities or needs to make new friends or keep up with old ones. Recall Betty Friedan's insistence that the suburbs were deliberately isolating for women, keeping them attached to the inner world of the home and cultivating a sense of loneliness and even despair. I can say from my own experience that living in the city pushed me out the door when I had a young child. Living in a tiny basement apartment with no yard to speak of, I spent every day in the summer at local parks, where meeting one mom turned into meeting five or six. Our friendships grew and gradually extended beyond time with the kids to include dinner, movies, parties, and more. The ease of being able to pop over to one another's houses kept us in constant contact.

At the same time I was trying to keep up with and in some cases re-establish my university friendships, and the city helped here even though my friends and I had very different experiences post-graduation and were embarking on new phases of life. We now lived in different neighbourhoods and our twenties and thirties were certainly not as carefree and energetic as those of Abbi and Ilana, nor nearly as glamourous as the aspirational lives of the *Sex and the City* girlfriends. Nonetheless, being a subway ride away made it feel like we could always find a way to get together, that maybe not so much had changed after all.

QUEER WOMEN'S SPACES

In the last decade or so, though, some of the most important urban spaces for women's friendships—those catering specifically to lesbian and queer women—have been lost. Historically, lesbians have struggled to find space in cities, as gay neighbourhoods typically focused on the interests and lifestyles of young gay men. Lesbian-friendly spaces like bars and bookshops have sometimes existed within these gay neighbourhoods. At other times, different streets would become informally known as lesbian-friendly zones, such as Commercial Drive in Vancouver and Boulevard St. Laurent in Montréal.[119] As Julie Podmore's research on Montréal suggests, "lesbian forms of territoriality at the urban scale have been relatively 'invisible' since their communities are constituted through *social networks* rather than commercial sites."[120] Friendship connections have been critical to the "lesbian grapevine" that helps queer women find streets and neighbourhoods that feel like home.

In Tamar Rothenberg's study of lesbian community in Park Slope, Brooklyn, entitled "'And she told two friends': Lesbians creating urban social space," particular places within Park Slope were important sites for lesbian recognition and sociality. These included the Seventh Avenue commercial district, where women described "the experience of walking down Seventh Avenue on a Saturday or Sunday, seeing lots of lesbians, running into people they know and feeling comfortable."[121] Geographer Gill Valentine also writes about the crucial importance of friendships among lesbians, who may have been rejected by family and other friends upon coming out. Lesbian friends become a surrogate family and take on many of the roles of care, support, celebration, and so on that are typically assumed by family of origin. In Valentine's study, women described the first visit to an explicitly lesbian venue as a kind of crossing over into a different world, one that took courage and nerve.[122]

Many of these neighbourhoods and venues were about to change, however. As early as the 1970s, Park Slope was beginning to see the effects of gentrification. Rising rents in Greenwich Village made Park Slope's old but attractive housing stock and relative proximity to Manhattan an appealing alternative. In a pattern familiar to observers of gentrification across dozens of different cities, the presence of alternative communities—students, artists, queer folks—seems to be a trigger for neighbourhood transitions from derelict to desirable. Ironically, those that made the neighbourhood "cool" in the first place are typically unable to afford to stay. With their relatively low household incomes thanks to the gendered wage gap and good old discrimination, lesbians are particularly vulnerable to displacement.

This trend has also affected commercial spaces like bars, cafés, and bookshops. In a recent video for *Xtra*, Toronto's queer news magazine, filmmaker and DJ Lulu Wei set out to investigate the complete disappearance of dedicated spaces for queer women in Toronto. How is this possible in a city with Canada's largest gay village and a world famous month-long Pride celebration that draws a million visitors? Wei interviews several former bar owners, promoters, and DJs who all point the finger at gentrification, income gaps, and a lack of welcoming spaces in the gay village. As DJ Cozmic Cat put it, "it's just a fact that two women together are going to have less income, disposable income, to drop at a club, to keep it open. And that's white women we're talking about, that's not even people of colour."[123] Pushed west because of high rents in the village, gentrification was close on their heels. As condos, boutiques, and mainstream bars appeared in these now "up-and-coming" neighbourhoods, queer women's spaces such as Less Bar and The Henhouse were shuttered.

Most of Wei's interviewees mourned the loss of these key community spaces. However, in a context where lesbian spaces and neighbourhoods have never been particularly abundant—even in the late 1990s, our favourite lesbian bar Slack Alice (later just Slack's) was the *only* women's bar in the village—queer women have always had to find ways to appropriate space.[124] DJ and promoter Mavis calls for "queer takeovers" of mainstream space. Bobby Valen, former owner of The Henhouse, says there *is* hope: "we all want something more, which is to be together . . . sometimes it *is* about taking space and not asking permission."[125] Although the nature of the places available has been deeply altered, lesbians and other queer women, trans and non-binary folks continue to find ways to make life-saving friendships and to create new kinds of creative and inclusive spaces as part of their urban survival toolkit.

FRIENDS 'TIL THE END

Queer or not, women's urban lives are changing. Women are getting married later in life and experiencing extended periods of independence in between leaving the family home and long-term partnerships. Increasing numbers of women are never getting married. In her powerful book *All the Single Ladies: Unmarried Women and the Rise of an Independent Nation*, Rebecca Traister praises the sustaining role of women's friendships and their rising importance: "Among the largely unacknowledged truths of female life is that women's primary, foundational, formative relationships are as likely to be with each other as they are with the men we've been told since childhood are supposed to be the people who complete us."[126]

Traister notes that our identities, dreams, and goals are being constructed alongside our friends rather than through the traditional pathways of marriage and family. Similarly, Schaefer acknowledges that her female friendships "are marked by all the signposts of romantic relationships, except they're platonic. But they are love stories . . . we're not letting the other person go."[127] In her foreword to her best friend and "work wife" Phoebe Robinson's book *You Can't Touch My Hair*, comedian Jessica Williams writes:

> She still refers to me as either her Oprah or her Gayle depending on what kind of day we are having. She still tells terrible dudes at bars that insist on having shitty conversations with us to *Please buzz off.* . . . Our first show together was like a great first date. I found out onstage that night that Phoebe was able to vocalize things that were deeply important to me. That being a black woman *and* a feminist is a full-time job. Like #fuckthepatriarchy even though we both usually date white dudes who look vitamin D deficient and probably burn in the sun too easily. That black lives do matter.[128]

Women's friendships are starting to be recognized for providing things that romantic partnership (especially with men) might not, such as a shared set of experiences and even a strong feminist foundation. And cities are providing the environments where women can make and sustain these connections, perhaps even over the course of a lifetime.

Even though those long nights of endless intimate talk are few and far between for my friends and I, we haven't stopped picturing our futures together. Sensing, perhaps, that most of us will outlive any men in our lives or that lifelong partnership may not be in the cards, and that relying on our post-millennial children to take care of us is probably not a solid plan, we often joke about soon reserving spaces in the same retirement home. Maybe our partners will be there, just in a separate wing. In my fantasies, it's like returning to university residence life with Kate and Jill, just fancier and a whole lot more relaxing.

We're not alone in having this vision. My social media feeds are full of young women (and men) professing their love for the *Golden Girls* with hashtags like #goals. Even though many of these folks are probably too young to have watched the brilliant sitcom during its original run, something about the lives of Dorothy, Blanche, Rose, and Sophia has gone from seeming like a sad consolation prize—spending your golden years living with your friends and mom in a retirement community—to, well, #goals. I can even imagine the *Sex and the City* friends living a New York version of the *Golden Girls* life together: Charlotte and Miranda's kids leave home; Mr. Big dies of a massive heart attack in the back of his town car; the women gather for longer and longer brunches in Miranda's Brooklyn brownstone until eventually, Steve moves into the basement and the friends just never leave. In real life, as Traister's research makes clear, the dream of growing old with a lifelong romantic partner either seems unrealistic, undesirable, or boring as hell. Instead, many people, women in particular, are fantasizing about an old age surrounded by friends and all of the care, support, fun, and adventure that friendships offer.

I don't know if this plan will ever come to fruition, but there's something world-making about imagining a future centred on female friendship. As Schaefer says, our girlfriends are "fundamental" to our lives and we're not giving them up. Instead, "we're reshaping the idea of what our public support systems are supposed to look like and what they can be."[129] But the retirement home fantasy is a rather privatized vision of a space where this is possible, one that relies on personal choices and the ability to pay. It doesn't necessarily require wider changes to social structures or the built environment. So the bigger question is how could we create or repurpose spaces, especially urban spaces, in ways that open up a wide range of possibilities for sustaining and practicing the kinds of relationships that we think will support us across the life course?

It's a challenging question with a lot of roadblocks in the way of an answer. Friendship, such a central preoccupation of childhood and adolescence, isn't taken as seriously in adulthood, and of course it exists in an informal and unstructured context. Unlike marriage, it's not recognized by the state and there are no formal or legal bonds of friendship. This is probably as it should be, but even without a "friendship license," adult friendships could be considered among the relationships and values important to the imagining of urban places. But it's particularly difficult when friendship is always contrasted with and then diminished in relation to "legitimate" connections such as those cemented by marriage, blood, or sexual intimacy.

It's also no secret that addressing households that don't align with the nuclear family model or "typical" life course—moving in a linear fashion from being single, to getting married, having kids, and finally being empty nesters—is rare in planning and city politics. As feminist planning critic Carolyn Whitzman notes, planning has long been a white, male-dominated profession.[130] Questions about gender, sexuality, and families are typically viewed as outside the rational, technical box ascribed to planning practice. Planner Deland Chan notes that "planning from below, and 'soft,' people-centered work like community outreach, aren't ascribed the same kind of value" as the work of designing the "hard" infrastructure of the city.[131] Gender mainstreaming approaches can help to accord greater value or at least draw attention to those concerns that have been ghettoized as "soft," not coincidentally because they're associated with women and femininity. Feminist urbanists claim that there's an "entrenched old guard wedded to old paradigms, uninterested in testing or exploring new ones" unless they involve fancy algorithms and big data.[132] Even within feminist geography, friendship has received very little attention as a "way of life" or a set of relationships and experiences that shapes and is shaped by the city.

If traditional heteropatriarchal household forms are rapidly diminishing as the norm in most people's lives, and certainly for large chunks of their lives, isn't it time we looked to other ways of being in relation to one another as the ground for shaping our urban futures? Given all of the ways that women rely on one another to provide not just the emotional support of friendship, but the very material support of shared childcare, elder care, transportation, housing, health care, and so many other completely necessary things, would it not make sense for cities to have the infrastructure to support such arrangements? Certainly we could make an economic argument around women's friendships. As Traister observes, women socializing together fill restaurants, bars, shops, and cafés from brunch until closing. She recalls moving to New York and watching women take up space together: "They—we actually—were sucking up every bit of energy from this city's sidewalks, populating its streets and its theatres and its office buildings and apartments, giving this city its character and its rhythm and its beauty and its speed."[133]

In my own research on Toronto's condo boom, I found that developers were marketing their buildings with images of this kind of 24/7 city of fun and friendship ideal.[134] However, this caters to a very privileged and quite narrow demographic of younger women professionals, mostly without children, who have disposable income and can use the city to enhance their lifestyle. It's still a long way from a city set up to nurture, enhance, and even rely on women's friendship networks as an integral and deeply necessary part of everyday life.

Over a hundred years ago, communal spaces for unmarried women, like Jane Addams' Hull House in Chicago, were built to keep young women out of trouble and safe in a seemingly hostile urban environment. While friendship wasn't the explicit basis for these homes, the notion that women would rely on one another, rather than individual men, for support, company, shared labour, education, and more was the prevailing ethos. Today, few such spaces exist and indeed barriers to making shared space abound. Co-owning property with a friend is unusual and often ill-advised; zoning practices may limit the number of "families" that can occupy a shared space; and condos and other multi-unit dwellings are often places where people live for short times, as they're not designed with the needs of different kinds of family shapes and sizes in mind, thus disrupting whatever networks might develop there. These restrictions, combined with high housing costs, can keep women trapped in untenable or even abusive relationships when they can't afford to move out of housing they share with a spouse or partner. The move to break up social housing projects into multi-income, mixed social and market housing neighbourhoods also messes with the supportive social networks that low-income women develop to help each other survive.

Ultimately, I don't think we can rely on urban policy and planning to sustain or generate the kinds of spaces that allow non-traditional relationships to flourish. Planning paradigms and property regimes that favour particular kinds of ownership are slow to change. Furthermore, in most cities, the private real estate market determines what kinds of spaces are built, which businesses survive, and even which services will be provided. As the example of disappearing places for queer women shows, the high costs of commercial spaces alongside gentrification are key factors shaping the possibilities for having and maintaining the kinds of sites that facilitate and nourish women's social networks and friendships. And although I think there's great wisdom and forethought in setting up society so that many different kinds of social relationships are in place as safety nets that can sustain us through illness, job loss, aging, etc., there's something radical, and therefore frightening, about women in particular finding ways to opt out of institutions such as marriage and even heterosexual monogamy itself.

The world-making endeavor of imagining a city of female friends is a little devious, even a little defiant. After all, if you've chosen a life in line with many of the tenets of heteronormativity (or homonormativity, for that matter), including marriage or long term commitment, property ownership, raising children, etc., what does it mean to fantasize about a point in your life when that central "core" of relationships and responsibilities drops into the background? Or even more radically, to realize that you can choose a life without any of those things and still have close, supportive, and deeply committed relationships throughout your whole life? We should never underestimate the power—and the threat—of challenging the centrality of the nuclear family, culturally, legally, and spatially.

Wunker insists that a focus on friendship has revolutionary potential. It defies patriarchal logics: "There are bodies with other bodies—laughing, crying, cooking, dancing, hugging—with no imperative to procreation or other reproductive labours. Friendship as counter to capitalist ideology. Friendship as its own economy."[135] Dakota scholar Kim TallBear suggests it might disrupt settler logics as well. TallBear speaks about hetero- and even homonormativity as part of the structure of "settler sexuality": ways of relating that value enforced monogamy, private property, and a particular set of relations with the state, which were imposed on Indigenous peoples and are part of the ongoing process of Indigenous dispossession.[136] Settler sexuality is thus part of the framework that stabilizes and normalizes the colonial state. It also denigrates the value of many other ways of being "in relation," including friendships, non-monogamy, relationships with the land, and relationships with non-humans. TallBear contends that these other ways of being in relation are profoundly destabilizing to colonial power structures.

Perhaps imagining the city centred on friendship seems impossible simply because of this: if women dedicated even a little bit more of their love, labour, and emotional support to their friend networks, the system—as men know it—would come crashing down. It's a radical prospect to consider, and one that profoundly decentres both the family and the state. TallBear insists:

I have radical hope that settler relations based on violent hierarchies and concepts of property do not have to be all there is.... We can have radical hope in a narrative that entails not redeeming the state, but caring for one another as relations. How do we live well here together? The state has and will continue to fail to help us do that.[137]

If women, Indigenous people, people of colour, queer, and trans folks insist on valuing and re-centring relations that have been systematically undermined, the status quo inevitably tilts in ways that are frightening and fantastic. This is a huge step toward the feminist city, the city that values women's relationships, decentres the nuclear family, and lets women and girls take up space and make relations on their own terms.

CHAPTER 3 **CITY OF ONE**

H ardly a week goes by without the appearance of yet another op-ed, thinkpiece, or viral meme decrying our addiction to mobile digital technologies. As in previous technology panics over the home television or the video game, we're warned that all of the attention we're giving to our personal tech is creating anti-social children, fomenting the breakdown of intimate relationships, making us more superficial and individualistic, and breaking the very bonds of civility and sociability that hold human societies together. Urban thinkers have hopped on this panic train too: according to some, our use of smartphones, digital music players, and other wearable tech is contributing to a more atomized, hostile urban environment where people don't participate in public social life.

In these visions, it's never clear who these social urban subjects are or what kinds of bodies they inhabit. These critiques both romanticize an imagined past when city streets were open and amiable, and envision a present where plucking those headphones out of our ears would create modern versions of the agora, with a multiplicity of spontaneous social interactions generating an urban renaissance. We're never told which magical spell banished sexism, racism, poverty, or homophobia from our civically-engaged streets. These rich fantasies certainly never consider that for some people, phones and headphones are part of our urban survival toolkit.

PERSONAL SPACE

Virginia Woolf wrote that "street haunting" in London was among the "greatest of pleasures."[138] Moving comfortably and silently through the city, drifting amongst fascinating strangers was a cherished pursuit. For women, however, being the flânuese is fraught. To enjoy being alone requires respect for personal space, a privilege that women have rarely been afforded. The idealized flâneur slips in and out of the urban crowd, one with the city yet also anonymous and autonomous.[139] Today, the flâneur might be blasting his favourite tunes through earbuds while strolling the city streets, enjoying his own personal urban adventure soundtrack.

I love having my headphones and music with me in the city too, but for me and many other women, they provide more than a form of entertainment. They may be small, but they create a social barrier against the all-too regular and almost always unwanted intrusions of men. It's impossible to know how many unwelcome conversations and incidents of street harassment I've avoided or been unaware of because of my headphones. I can, however, think of times when a little set of white earbuds might have saved me from humiliating and deeply sexist encounters.

I recall walking home one afternoon from a day shift at the pub where I worked in North London. A man sitting in a parked car waved me over. Because he was stopped in an odd place (and because I'm a helpful Canadian), I assumed he wanted directions. In fact, he wanted to perform oral sex on me. His words were less polite. I can't remember what, if anything, I said back to him, but I walked the rest of the way home shaking and looking over my shoulder, afraid that he could easily follow me to my empty house.

Here I was, trying to be a good urban citizen. I helpfully emerged from the quiet bubble of a nice walk home after my bartending job, which involved hours of enforced chit-chat with inebriated men, to assist a stranger. Encounters like this can only diminish my sympathy for those who yearn for an illusory past filled with neighbourly sociability on the streets. For many, this has never been part of the urban experience. For us, the ability to be alone is an equally important marker of a successful city. The extent to which violations of women's personal space via touch, words, or other infringements are tolerated and even encouraged in the city is as good a measure as any for me of how far away we actually are from the sociable—and feminist—city of spontaneous encounters.

This gaping distance hit me recently when an article entitled *How to Talk to a Woman Wearing Headphones* was blasted across social media.[140] Written by a man who seems to identify as a pick-up artist, the article started to circulate in August 2016 and sent my feminist-heavy Twitter timeline into a meltdown. The author begins by insisting even "crazy feminists" "will pretty much instantly melt and be nice when a confident guy walks up and says hello," so men shouldn't hesitate to *repeatedly* ask a woman to remove her headphones. He assures his male readers that no matter what signals women give, they secretly always want men to interrupt whatever they're doing. In fact, the article suggests that men should persist even when women show obvious signs of disinterest.

Instant social media critiques of the advice article were often humorous, like this tweet from Amy Elizabeth Hill: "I'm just a girl wearing headphones standing in front of a boy asking him to fucking move out of my way because I don't want to talk to him" (@amyandelizabeth, August 30, 2016). Others used more traditional media outlets to provide incisive breakdowns of all the ways this advice perpetuates rape culture. For example, Martha Mills responded in *The Guardian* by evoking the escalating sense of fear that women feel when approached repeatedly, when our signals are ignored or misconstrued, and when our boundaries are violated. She explains, "My brain is in fight or flight, checking for escape routes, it's trying to figure out just how aggressively you're going to react to any further action I take to extract myself from a situation entirely not of my own making." Making the connection to rape culture, Mills goes on to note "the advice here is basically 'No doesn't mean no, it means keep going until you get what you want—the screaming will stop eventually.' Because apparently that's what women want."[141]

How to Talk to a Woman Wearing Headphones illustrates (some) men's inability to acknowledge that women have the desire or the right to exist in public space by themselves, for themselves. It's unfathomable to the author and his supporters that women do not constantly, if secretly, crave the attention of men. They're incapable of understanding that every such interaction is coloured by the enormous baggage of rape culture and a lifetime of contradictory gendered socialization: beware of strangers, but also, always be nice to strange men.

This paradox was heartbreakingly illustrated by the murder of Mollie Tibbetts in July 2018. Jogging alone near her home in Brooklyn, Iowa, Tibbetts was murdered after she reportedly tried to ignore a man's attempts to speak to her. The suspect seems to have a history of repeatedly harassing women who reject his advances. While much of the media focused on the immigration status of the accused, feminists have spoken out about the onslaught of harassment that women face. After CNN cited a *Runner's World*[142] study on harassment with a headline claiming that a "startling number of women say they have been harassed while running,"[143] women on social media responded with incredulity: "Startling to whom?" tweeted actress June Diane Raphael (@MsJuneDiane, August 23, 2018). Women cyclists also report sexual harassment in addition to (or layered throughout) the threats they receive as cyclists daring to take up space on the road.[144] Not only is this kind of harassment routine, it's dangerous. Women are told to ignore this obnoxious behavior, but when we do, we risk sudden and even extreme levels of violence.

In this cultural environment, being alone is a luxury for women, and one we rarely get to enjoy for long. We're always anticipating the next approach from a stranger and we have no way of knowing whether that interaction will be benign or threatening. Wearing headphones is one way that women can attempt to claim their personal space but even this little symbol of independence is easily ignored. For women, anonymity and invisibility are always temporary and must be jealously guarded. I'd love to live in a city of friendly, spontaneous social encounters too; but until I feel confident that men will respect my autonomy and safety, I won't apologize for wearing my anti-social earbuds.

TABLE FOR ONE

It takes an enormous amount of mental energy to navigate the public and private spaces of the city alone as a woman. In an episode of *Sex and the City*, the normally confident Samantha finds herself stood up at a fancy restaurant. She feels humiliated and ashamed that she was forced to sit alone, withering under the pitying stares of other customers. Her anger at being stood up is secondary to the embarrassment Samantha experiences under the microscope of the public gaze. A man dining alone might be perceived as a business traveler or simply a confident person. He is unlikely to be harassed or pitied. A woman dining alone feels out of place, on display, and kind of sad. On the show, writer Carrie wonders why this has to be the case. She challenges herself to go out for a meal by herself, with no book or newspaper for company (the show takes place before smartphones existed). Nothing dramatic happens, but Carrie's trepidation illustrates how deeply fraught the choice to go alone for a simple meal can become.

The constant calculations and final "gut checks" associated with going out alone are difficult enough in your home city, but even more challenging when travelling. In 2015 I was doing research in Chicago and Atlanta and I had to spend most of my time alone in those cities, where I had few friends and research meet-ups didn't take up my whole days. At least once a day and usually more I had to venture alone into a bar or restaurant for a meal. Sometimes I'd plan ahead of time, looking at pictures and reviews on Google. I was curious about the menu and prices, of course, but more often I was searching for a clue about a category that isn't (but maybe should be?) included in a normal review: is this a comfortable place for a woman to sit in alone?

After the online search came the walk-by. This was also part of my routine for more "spontaneous" finds when I was already out and about. Sometimes the walk-by was actually three or four walk-bys, trying to get a glimpse inside through darkened windows or curtains. Were there lots of people in there? Was anyone else alone? Did the bartenders look friendly? The moment of entering is most stressful. Am I brave enough to turn around and walk out if I feel awkward? Am I also brave enough to walk up to the bar and take a seat? Sometimes I haven't even been brave enough to walk in, settling instead for fast food and Netflix. But as an urban researcher (and someone who likes a decent meal) I can't hide away in my hotel room every time I go out to do research or travel for a conference. I confess that once I find a neighbourhood pub that feels comfortable, I often return multiple times. It's simply too much work and stress to scout out a new location for every meal. Again, I seem to be failing at the urban adventure.

I'm certain I'm not alone in feeling anxiety and second guessing myself when it comes to seemingly basic choices like where to grab a veggie burger at the end of the day. The anxiety isn't even necessarily related to fear of men or physical harm. Rather, it's a calculation made to figure out how likely my personal boundaries are to be respected at any given time. As a woman, the privilege of being able to mind my own business is a rare one. It's also true that I can't predict when a benign interaction will turn into a threat, which means that I have to be guarded. This daily reality paints a dismal picture of urban living, one that undermines so many visions of the "good" urban life.

Influential and much beloved critic of planning Jane Jacobs wrote about city neighbourhoods where a 24/7 liveliness and an engaged community meant that people would feel comfortable using the streets.[145] She believed that the ability to feel safe while alone amongst millions of strangers was the ultimate marker of a city's livability. Jacobs famously wrote about "eyes on the street" as an expression of this engagement and constant mixed use. However, she didn't mean the eyes of state surveillance, CCTV, policing, or harassment. Nor did she mean kinds of "eyes" that police things like gender expression, sexuality, or the behavior of racialized minorities and youth. Too often however, the idea of "eyes on the street" has led to coercive forms of surveillance and harassment that make it impossible to be safe and alone among strangers.

Black and Indigenous people and people of colour are routinely viewed with suspicion in public places and are often interrogated about their presence, or worse. In April 2018, two Black men were arrested after a Philadelphia Starbucks manager called the police because they hadn't yet purchased anything. They were simply waiting for their friend to arrive. When he showed up a few minutes late, they were already in handcuffs. The men were taken to a police station and held for nine hours before being released without charge.[146] The arrest was filmed and the viral video led to public outcry and apologies from Starbucks. In the wake, author Teju Cole reflected via Facebook on what this means for Black people in public:

> We are not safe even in the most banal place. We are not equal even in the most common circumstances. We are always five minutes away from having our lives upended.... This is why I always say you can't be a black flâneur. Flânerie is for whites. For blacks in white terrain, all spaces are charged. Cafés, restaurants, museums, shops. Your own front door. This is why we are compelled, instead, to practice psychogeography. We wander alert, and pay a heavy psychic toll for that vigilance. Can't relax, black (Teju Cole, Facebook, April 18, 2018).

The incident is an extreme version of the microaggressions Black people face in public, such that being alone requires a constant state of vigilance and self-surveillance. Toronto journalist

Desmond Cole, in his raw *Toronto Life* essay on his experiences of being "carded"[147] by police, writes about the "psychic toll" of regular police and citizen surveillance of Black people:

> I have come to accept that some people will respond to me with fear or suspicion—no matter how irrational it may seem. After years of needless police scrutiny, I've developed habits to check my own behaviour. I no longer walk through upscale clothing stores like Holt Renfrew or Harry Rosen, because I'm usually tailed by over-attentive employees. If I'm paying cash at a restaurant, I will hand it to the server instead of leaving it on the table, to make sure no one accuses me of skipping out on the bill.[148]

These examples illustrate how white privilege is bound up with the privilege of enjoying being alone. People of colour are made to feel like trespassers or criminals in their own cities, risking harassment, arrest, and even violent death for simple acts like hanging out at Starbucks or asking to use a public washroom. As Teju Cole says, the Black flâneur is an impossibility under white supremacy.

Disabled people experience a different kind of interference in their right to be alone. They often find themselves accosted by (mostly) well- meaning but ignorant strangers who insist on "helping" without asking for consent. This help typically involves unwanted physical contact such as taking hold of a wheelchair or grabbing the arm of a blind person to guide them. Wheelchair user Bronwyn Berg recounts the terrifying experience of having her wheelchair grabbed from behind by a stranger who began pushing her along a busy street in Nanaimo, where passersby ignored her cries for help.[149] Visually impaired activist Amy Kavanagh launched a campaign called #JustAskDontGrab after she began using a white cane and found people grabbing her on her London commute. Not only is this intrusive and rude, it may lead to injury. Moreover, it's often an expression of impatience or thinly veiled hostility. Wheelchair user Gabrielle Peters recalls the time a taxi driver pushed her rapidly towards the cab, causing her to tip out of her chair onto the pavement. Like Berg, Kavanagh wants disabled people to be asked for their consent before being touched and to have their bodily autonomy respected. Berg says, "Our assistive devices are a part of our body. We aren't furniture that can be moved around."[150] It's bad enough that the urban environment is full of physical barriers; Berg notes that after her chair was grabbed, she couldn't enter a shop to ask for help because of the steps outside. The lack of respect for basic personal boundaries makes it extra challenging for disabled people to exercise their right to move about urban public space in whatever ways they want or need to.

THE RIGHT TO BE ALONE

Being with friends in the city allowed me, as a teenager and young woman, to take up space, experiment with identities, be different, be loud, be myself. Friends are so important to this because while alone, women engage in all kinds of self-policing in order to avoid unwanted attention and hostile surveillance of their bodies and behaviours. It's still incredibly difficult for women alone to actually take up space. Think of the difference in body language and posture of a woman riding the subway versus the ubiquitous "man-spreader" who sits down and opens his legs so wide that he either occupies more than one seat or forces those around him to curl up into themselves. Women are socialized not to take up space, especially as individuals. The best we hope for is to slip under the radar.

However, there's more to this quest for being alone than avoiding harassment. Walking along a city street or sitting alone in a crowded café is an especially delicious kind of alone time for women. I really noticed this when I became a mother and had the occasional opportunity to be out by myself. There were people all around me, but none of them had a right to demand my emotional labour. In fact, some were even taking care of me: bringing me coffee, cleaning my table. It was delightful to be out in public and realize that I didn't have to respond in any way to a child's whines or incessant questions. Perhaps being alone while out in the city is so precious for women because at home we're always in demand.

The gendered expectations around parenting, domestic labour, household management, relationships, pets, and more mean that the family home is rarely a place where women can have solitary moments. Like other moms, I have plenty of stories of being regularly interrupted on the toilet or in the shower. Even in these most private of spaces intrusions are expected. It's surprisingly common for sleep-deprived moms to stay up well after the household goes to bed. A blogger and father of three small children shared his epiphany that his wife was extra exhausted because late nights were the only time she had to herself. The mom in the story tells her husband that she has "sensory overload" from constant touching, noise, and demands from the kids. After they go to bed, she spends time with her husband but has absolutely no time to be alone until he also goes to bed. She would rather sacrifice sleep for a few hours in which she can just be.[151] In addition to nocturnal "me time," many moms find that the only way to guarantee time alone is to leave the house altogether.

It's deeply pleasurable to pull out a novel or magazine while sitting in a café or bar, or on a park bench, particularly when it's an escape from the demands of home or work. Even working alone in public is sometimes a treat. The change of setting and background din can be productive elements for writing, editing, and planning research. Even grading papers can feel less daunting. If I lived in a city, I'd almost certainly be writing this book in a variety of my favourite coffee shops.

The rareness of time away from domestic demands and the general overload of gendered relational labour and care work makes intrusions even more annoying. I know that the simple act of sitting and reading in a public space will eventually draw the attention of a man who wants to know what I'm reading. Of course, I'm never interrupted when I sit to study or write with a man. The conundrum is this: a woman alone is presumed always available to other men. It links back to notions of women as men's property. If a woman out in public isn't clearly marked as property by the presence of another man or obvious signals such as wedding rings (which of course may symbolize non-heterosexual unions as well), then she is fair game. Women instinctively know that the quickest way to deter a man's unwanted advances is to tell him that you have a boyfriend or husband. Men will respect another man's property rights more readily than they'll respect a woman's simple "no."

Jane Darke, who posited that the city is "patriarchy written in stone," goes on to say that women are made to feel like "guests" at best in the city, knowing that they're effectively in men's territory and could be seen as trespassing if they do not "comport themselves in particular ways." Darke wearily notes the regular calls of "cheer up love!" directed at women alone.[152] I've been told (commanded?) to "smile!" by countless men as I try to go about my business in the city. I've been admonished to be more "lady-like" when calling out men's rude behaviour. If I'm not smiling, and therefore indicating that I'm nice, submissive, eager to please men, then I'm a bitch or a cow or a dyke. Some might say that it's not sexist for a man to tell a woman to smile, but can you imagine a man telling another man on the street to smile?

Erin Wunker opens *Notes from a Feminist Killjoy* with the statement: "I have a bitchy resting face."[153] She rues the automatic grimace-y smile that gets triggered like a reflex when she's told to smile. A reflex honed under patriarchy, sharpened within rape culture. For lots of us, this "smile" reflex eventually morphs into a "giving the finger" reflex, a true killjoy stance. A woman who isn't smiling is a woman who is in her own thoughts, has her own agenda, isn't there to simply please men or be an object for their gaze. A woman or non-binary person or gender-fluid person who isn't chasing particular standards of femininity isn't there to please or appease heterosexual men. Therefore, they're threats. They don't belong. They're not behaving like property.

WOMEN IN PUBLIC

The notion of women as property and restrictions on women being alone in urban public space have a long history. Elizabeth Wilson discusses the moral panic surrounding women's increased visibility on the city streets in Victorian London. The term "public woman" is of course an old euphemism for a sex worker. The idea that women of status could somehow be mistaken for poor women or sex workers was cause for much hand-wringing and the reassertion of the need for women to be chaperoned by their husbands, brothers, fathers, or older women.[154]

Women's increased desire for independence in the city ushered in the era of the department store in Paris in the 1870s, a setting that was literally designed to be an appropriate public space for women. It would limit their contact with the unsavoury elements of the street but also allow them a measure of the freedom they so keenly sought. Émile Zola's 1883 novel *Au Bonheur des Dames* (The Ladies' Paradise) offers a glimpse behind the scenes of a fictional store based on the first department store in Paris.[155] Amidst the intrigues of the shopgirls, the owner's love life, and the politics of a big business competing against local shops, Zola's book shows how spectacles of consumption were designed to delight women's senses. Spaces of shopping were thus amongst the first spaces where women (in the west at least) were permitted to claim public space.

Feminist geographers Liz Bondi and Mona Domosh write about the gendered patterning of city spaces in mid-nineteenth century New York City, drawing on the diary of a middle-class visitor to the city, Sophie Hall.[156] Although always accompanied by a woman friend during her daytime activities, Sophie's detailed record of her visit illustrates how areas of the city were gendered in ways that allowed for some moderate freedoms for white women. For example, the "Ladies' Mile" centred along Broadway and Sixth between Tenth and Twenty-third was the "city's new consumer showpiece," a public space that was considered "appropriately feminine." Districts that included museums and art galleries were also part of Sophie's itinerary. Again, these were activities "sanctioned by Victorian standards" and settings that "had been patterned to make them safe and appropriate for women."[157]

The late nineteenth-century industrial order required not only a commitment to production and hard work, it required a commitment to values of consumption. The gendering of "separate spheres" meant that production could be aligned with the world of men and consumption with the world of women. Women's active participation in consumption activities, however, challenged the notion that their proper place was confined to the home and meant that women would need access to typically masculine spaces of the city in order to fulfill their roles as consumers. Lest this be too disruptive to Victorian norms, this change was "neutralized by the development in the nineteenth century of 'feminized' consumer spaces within the city—if women had to be on the streets of the masculine city, then those streets and stores had to be designed as 'feminine.'"[158] Importantly, this meant that women's white bourgeois identities could be safely reinforced through their visibility in these spaces of proper femininity.

These spaces of consumption were open to women because in many ways they didn't challenge women's association with the home and the domestic sphere. By shopping for clothing, décor, and art, women were fulfilling their roles as caretakers of the hearth. Still today, a woman alone in these public spaces is properly "tethered" to the home. Even if she's shopping for herself, or indulging in what we like to call "self-care" activities, her alone-ness doesn't disrupt the normative gender order. The body, the intimate, self-care, and aesthetics are normatively women's realms.

While standards for proper femininity have loosened somewhat since Victorian times, the range of places where women can be comfortably alone without seeming "out of place" isn't so different. Although women today aren't as restricted as dear Sophie Hall, who wasn't even allowed to be seen eating or drinking in public, spaces of consumption, culture, and entertainment are still considered the most appropriate venues for women's public lives. When I studied condominium development in Toronto, I analyzed hundreds of condo advertisements in terms of their gendered imagery. Images of women shopping, eating, drinking, and socializing were much more common than images of women going to work. There was a strong *Sex and the City* vibe to many of the ads: the excitement of city life for women was cast in terms of their access to the 24/7 leisure- and consumption-scape of downtown Toronto and other "up and coming" neighbourhoods.[159]

Bondi and Domosh compare the freedoms and restrictions experienced by Sophie Hall on her 1879 New York trip to the experiences of Moira MacDonald, a divorced middle-class white woman from Edinburgh whom Bondi interviewed in 1991. While Moira has a professional job, owns her own home, and lives alone in a desirable, gentrifying neighbourhood, she feels constraints on her ability to comfortably access public spaces of the city. Despite a strong belief in gender equality at work and in the home, Moira doesn't question the gendered norm that unmonitored city spaces (such as parks) are "imbued with a hostile masculinity" and thus are not safe spaces for her to be alone.[160] Moira and Sophie share the need to adapt their behavior to their sense of gendered vulnerability.

Although today women are much more free to move within these spaces in the same ways as men (depending of course on social class and race), women remain acutely aware that to be alone outside of these "sanctioned" spaces is to be made vulnerable to unwanted attention and the threat of violence. As Bondi and Domosh note, "the public spaces of late-twentieth-century western cities are spaces of commercial consumer activities" that are "surveyed to create environments in which middle-class, feminine identities are fostered and protected," much as the shopping spaces of the nineteenth century were.[161] In this context, we can see that the freedom offered to women by contemporary city life is still bound by gendered norms about the proper spaces and roles of women in the city.

The feminization of urban space continues today. As global north cities have transitioned away from economies based on industrial manufacturing to economies based on knowledge and service work (so-called post-industrial economies), the more masculinized features of cities have changed. Spaces such as pubs, once either closed to women or gender segregated, have "softened" many of their more masculine attributes to appeal to women customers. Even donut shops (such as Canada's Tim Hortons) and fast food restaurants such as McDonald's have altered their aesthetics to embrace a homey, café quality suitable for families rather than truck drivers.[162] Changes to colour schemes, layouts, business names, furniture, and menus (more salads = more women!) alter the atmosphere to make them seem comfortable and safe for women. Geographers have linked these changes with gentrification, observing that working class sports bars and diners are closing and being replaced by "hipper" (and whiter) middle-class spaces without strong gender associations attached.

In one of my old neighbourhoods in Toronto—the Junction—I experienced firsthand how a formerly industrial, working class area was gentrifying through the rise of feminized spaces that stood in stark contrast to the traditionally masculine spaces that had once dominated the area. Greasy diners, porn shops, pawn shops, and bars that catered to a mostly male, working class clientele were gradually replaced by yoga studios, nail salons, cafés, and organic grocery stores.[163]

When I first moved to the Junction in early 2000, Dundas Street hosted few places that I'd have ventured into alone to have a coffee or a drink. Not because they were dangerous, but because they were clearly not catering to me as a young woman.

And that's okay—the neighbourhood didn't need to conform to my desires! But the Junction is an interesting example of how cities and neighbourhoods use women's comfort, pleasure, and safety as markers of successful revitalization. Indeed, women's lack of comfort in certain spaces can be used as justification for a host of problematic interventions that increase danger for others, for example homeless people and people of colour, in the pursuit of comfort for middle-class white women. In the Junction, the first sign of this feminization was the opening of a narrow little coffee shop called The Nook that had a small play area for children in the back.

The Nook was a clear example of what urban sociologists have called "a third place."[164] These are places that are neither home nor work, but are essential informal gathering spaces for communities. In her study of how Canadian urban dwellers understand their own use of specialty coffee shop chains such as Starbucks and Second Cup as urban spaces, sociologist Sonia Bookman notes that some consumers describe these cafés as "home away from home."[165] With a variety of soft furnishings, fireplaces, bookshelves, small tables for intimate conversation, and a general sense of hospitality, these cafés are quasi-public home spaces for many. It's perhaps then not surprising that such cafés are places where women out alone feel welcome, comfortable, and reasonably safe. As "third places," cafés carefully cultivate an environment (and of course a brand) where people can be alone, together. Given the long-standing restrictions on women's ability to be alone in public, coffee shops are places where women can experience, in relative safety, the psychic pleasures of urban life: being anonymous in a crowd, people watching, taking up space, being alone with your thoughts while surrounded by others.

The increasing numbers of "feminized" quasi-public, quasi-home places like The Nook and the eventual (inevitable?) arrival of a Starbucks in the Junction were clear signs of gentrification. Spaces I'd once avoided—the donut shop with its parking lot full of men sitting on their cars smoking, greasy diners, sports bars—began to close their doors. Parents with expensive strollers ambled along the dirty pavements and soon the sounds of construction filled the air as condo developers found a ripe new market. It's not lost on me that this transformation was in service of the preferences and desires of women like myself. And the link between a class transformation of city spaces and making them safer for women seems to have been accepted as common sense by developers, planners, and other boosters of "revitalization." Of course, this assumption has an image of a particular kind of woman at its centre: a white, able-bodied, middle-class, cis woman.

In the Junction, the limits of this vision were made clear via the experiences of women who resided for short-to-medium term stays at the Salvation Army's Evangeline Women's Shelter. These women experience serious, chronic poverty, even amidst the revitalization of the area.[166] Their presence gradually became more and more out of place on the neighbourhood's sidewalks as gentrification encroached. Often forced to be alone in public by shelter rules that don't allow them to stay inside all day, these women don't easily experience the pleasure of being alone in the crowd. Rather than enjoying some people watching, the women from the shelter find themselves watched constantly. Their physical appearance, habits, and occasional expressions of mental illness mark them as "other," even though the shelter has existed for many years and the Junction has long been home to a wide variety of poor, working class, disabled, or otherwise "different" folks.

In one example of how the simple act of being alone in public was made more difficult for the shelter's residents, a café next door to the shelter removed an outside bench because customers complained that women from the shelter sat there to smoke. Although the café owner was sympathetic to the women in the shelter and engaged in supportive projects like providing holiday meals, she was pressured by the gentrifiers who frequented the café to "clean up" the space.[167] This eliminated one spot where the women could safely be alone in public. In other cases, outward signs of trauma or mental illness exhibited by women were the subject of nasty diatribes by other community members debating the benefits of gentrification in the neighbourhood via online community forums. Terms like "freak show" conveyed the hostility that some demonstrate towards women who don't always behave in normative ways. These examples are reminders that as much as the freedom for some women to be alone in public has improved, the policing of others and the removal of safe spaces has simultaneously increased.

TOILET TALK

One of those spaces that has both been highly limited in its availability and highly policed is the public or publicly accessible bathroom. When we think of urban public space, bathrooms aren't likely to come to mind, and in fact this is at the heart of the problem. As a space where we want and often need to be alone, in a most pressing and sometimes urgent manner, the bathroom—or lack of a bathroom—generates all kinds of questions about safety, accessibility, gender, sexuality, class, homelessness, race, and more.

Like a lot of other issues, bathroom access became visible to me as an urban concern when I had an infant and then a toilet-training toddler in tow. I quickly learned that department stores were our best bet for emergency diaper changes, spots to nurse, and a decent level of cleanliness and provisioning. As spaces built with the comfort of women in mind, department stores, while not always explicitly set up to best serve mothers, were spaces where the bathrooms were likely to be spacious, have lots of stalls, be elevator or escalator accessible, have a chair one could sit in to nurse, offer baby changing stations, be a safe space to leave a stroller outside, and so on. On particularly messy outings, they were also places I could buy a quick change of clothes to replace a poop-splattered onesie. In fact, department stores remain my go-to places to "go" whether I have a kid with me or not. Unfortunately, urban department stores are disappearing, and with them their comfortable and accessible bathrooms.

Outside of the reasonably comfortable world of "The Ladies' Paradise," the quest for good places to go in the city is daunting. In *No Place to Go: How Public Toilets Fail Our Private Needs*, journalist and writer Lezlie Lowe asks, "Why are public toilets so crappy?"[168] Recalling her own experiences of facing "public" bathrooms that were locked, down steep flights of stairs, filthy, dangerous, and long distances from main streets and activity centres, Lowe investigates the history of how and why cities have, or have not, made public bathrooms a priority. Lowe notes that in the Victorian period, growing cities recognized a need for urban restrooms; however, these weren't at all attentive to the needs of women, children, or disabled people. Over time, though, cities increasingly relied on private or quasi-private entities— department stores, government institutions, cafés, etc.—to provide these spaces. As most of us know, though, these spaces rarely guarantee access and indeed may be protected by security guards, payment machines, and door codes designed to limit who can enter and what activities can happen. The ordeal that the two Black customers faced in Starbucks began, apparently, when one asked for a bathroom key before either had made a purchase. Having to ask permission to access a space for one of the most basic and universal human needs led to a situation that could have ended in the injury or death of either man.

Bathroom needs and access are also deeply gendered issues. Some of these issues have to do with the complex mix of biological and cultural factors that shape how people with different body parts use the bathroom. For most women, relieving ourselves takes longer, will regularly involve addressing menstruation needs, and requires the removal or major adjustment of clothing. We need more toilet paper, places to hang coats and purses, stalls with doors, and are more likely to be responsible for helping with the bathroom needs of babies, children, disabled people, or elderly family members. Yet as Lowe points out, most public bathrooms fail miserably at acknowledging and serving these needs.

In part, this problem stems from fact that most architects and planners are men who have taken little time to really consider what women might want or need in a restroom. But it also has to do with taboos around talking about "bathroom stuff" and in particular menstruation. Lowe writes that menstruation "has been almost perfectly unknowable to the (mostly) cisgender men designing and installing bathrooms in public buildings and public spaces."[169] No one wants to talk about blood, sanitary products, or the need for clean and comfortable places to perform basic menstruation care. No one wants to acknowledge that bathroom use takes longer when menstruating, causes more frequent urination, includes cramping that can lead to urgent bowel movements, and can include "flooding" that needs to be dealt with immediately. No one wants to recognize that some trans men might also need products and facilities to deal with menstruation. No one wants to help homeless women by addressing both the cost of pads and tampons as well as the lack of freely accessible bathroom space in cities (although a major drug store chain in Canada will soon offer boxes with free menstrual products for women in need).

Around the world women have taken action to assert their rights to equitable and appropriate access to bathrooms. Women like Clara Greed and Susan Cunningham in the U.K. and Joan Kuyek in Canada have become known as "toilet ladies" for their work pushing to put bathroom access on the agendas of governments, planners, builders, and architects. In New Delhi settlements, women community leaders advocate for sanitation to become a local priority, noting that women wait in lines for upwards of twenty minutes each time they queue to use the only facilities available: public toilets. In India more generally, toilet access has been central to women's activism against sexual assault. The shocking rape and murder of two girls who'd gone into a field to relieve themselves at night in 2014 sparked nationwide protests and drew global attention to a long standing problem: the lack of safe facilities for women and girls put them at even greater risk of violence. Sharmila Murthy explains:

> An estimated 2.5 billion people globally lack access to proper sanitation, with the largest number living in India.... Many poor women living in rural villages or urban slums wait until nightfall, reducing their food and drink intake so as to minimize the need for elimination. Girls often do not attend school if there are no private toilets, and this is especially true after the onset of menstruation. Approximately 2,200 children die every day as a result

of diarrheal diseases linked to poor sanitation and hygiene, which impacts women as mothers and caregivers. Finally, waiting until nighttime to urinate or defecate is not only dehumanizing, it makes women vulnerable to sexual assault.[170]

The United Nations has recognized sanitation as both a women's rights issue and a human rights issue, but little progress has been made on this particular development goal.

Trans people have been pushed to the frontlines of toilet activism by the exclusion, danger, and violence they often face in trying to use an appropriate facility at work, school, and in public buildings.[171] Lowe writes: "If there's any revolution happening in public bathrooms now, it's being driven by the transgender community."[172] While disability advocates succeeded in making changes to the physical form of bathrooms such that accessible stalls, sinks, and doors are mandatory features of all new buildings, trans people are at the forefront of what will likely be the next big change in bathroom access: the partial desegregation of bathrooms by gender and the rise of more single user, all-gender/gender-free toilets.

My university residence had co-ed multi-stall washrooms and shower facilities back in the 1990s. It took a day or two to get used to the sight of a dude strolling up to the sink in boxers or coming out of the shower stall. The few problems we had couldn't be attributed to gender differences. The gender of the person who pooped on the floor *right next* to a toilet one long weekend was never discovered, for example. Yet this kind of fully desegregated arrangement remains extremely rare. Binary gender segregated washrooms are the norm, and the formal and informal policing of who enters each space means that trans folks as well as anyone else who doesn't conform to strict gender norms approaches this basic daily need with stress, fear, and the looming threat of harassment and violence. The bogeyman figure of the cis man who dresses like a woman to enter women's washrooms in order to spy on or assault women has been used as a perverse justification for trying to determine the genitals of anyone using a gender-segregated bathroom. If cis men actually had to spend enough time getting into drag that they passed as women in order to sexually assault women, I suspect there would be a lot less sexual assault. I'm not making light of actual violence here. Rather, I think the fear of "fake" trans women is rooted purely in transphobia, and not in any actual concern for the real violence that women—trans and cis—experience regularly.

Some public institutions such as university campuses and businesses with publicly accessible washrooms have begun to make single-stall washrooms gender-free, a move that certainly makes sense and requires few resources beyond new signage and perhaps sanitary item disposal units. However, converting all bathrooms into single-user spaces is costly and inefficient, space-wise. It's likely to lead to long line ups and may disadvantage people with disabilities that require more immediate access to facilities. Converting all multi-stall bathrooms into gender-free spaces can be problematic for people with religious restrictions. In short, there's no single solution that can come entirely from changes to our built forms. Like so many other issues in cities and beyond, social changes are also required. Single stalls won't eliminate transphobia or end gender-based violence. In the meantime, however, ensuring the greatest possible bathroom access for all bodies across gender, ability, and class is a necessary step in creating a feminist city.

WOMEN TAKING UP SPACE

The limitation that accompanies an inability to know you can relieve yourself in the city is just one more reason why I don't wax nostalgic for an urban street life that either didn't exist or was limited to a privileged few. Instead of romanticizing a time before earbuds and smartphones and smartwatches, I prefer to imagine a city where a woman can wear her headphones without fear of intrusion or choose not to wear headphones at all with the same result. In some cases, portable technologies are innovative tools that allow women to assert their presence in urban space. Feminist geographer Ayona Datta noticed that women research participants in slum resettlement colonies outside Delhi were "avid selfie takers." Datta theorizes,

> the selfies show that being in the city is liberating for women, as they represent a new-found freedom outside the home and the constraints of traditional gender roles. Through these selfies, women curate the city at arm's length, placing themselves in the centre of the frame as they stage their own arrival in many different public places.[173]

With or without portable technologies, I'm not fantasizing about a city where everyone walks around in a little bubble, snapping selfies, having minimal interaction with other humans, non-humans, and the environment itself. Rather, I'm suggesting that the freedom to do so in comfort, safety, and autonomy is foundational to the kind of city where people will *want* to socialize with one another and interact fully with the environment. Imagining this freedom for women also compels us to attend to other groups who routinely have their right to simply exist in public violated and aggressively policed.

The right to take up space is where the pleasure of being alone meets a wider politics of gender and power. Being socialized to go unnoticed affects women's inclination (or lack thereof) to take up public roles and voice their opinions, whether that's through running for political office, becoming a professor, or being vocal on the Internet. This socialization is then aggressively reinforced by the misogynist discourse faced by women who do dare to stand up as individuals. Alberta's former Premier Rachel Notley, for example, is regularly targeted for harassment based on her gender rather than her policies (or rather, these get conflated: her "bad" policies are the result of her gender). Misogyny clearly played a role in the negative press coverage and lack of support among many for Hillary Clinton's presidential campaign. These women are seen as fair game for such attacks because they have dared to *be* noticed. Women like Anita Sarkeesian and Lindy West who put their (feminist) opinions out on social media are told that they should expect and just accept violent insults, rape threats, and even in-person harassment as "natural" responses to voicing their thoughts and taking up virtual space.[174] This is intimately connected to the local, urban scale, where everyday women who insist on taking up public space are also seen as fair game for harassment and even violence. In this way, restrictions—self-imposed and otherwise—on women in public have far-reaching implications and connections to other forms of gendered oppression and inequality.

Earlier in this chapter, I wrote about the two Philadelphia men who were arrested while waiting for their friend at Starbucks. In the intervening two or three weeks since typing that paragraph and this conclusion, stories broke about a parent calling the police on two Native American men on a campus tour because they were "too quiet;" a white woman calling the police on a Black woman student at Yale who had fallen asleep in a study room; and neighbours calling the police on Black women checking out of an Airbnb because they assumed they were stealing. I could list more, all from the last two to three weeks. It's glaringly obvious that people of colour are routinely viewed as trespassers in the city. Just as patriarchy is enshrined in the urban environment, white supremacy is also the ground upon which we walk.

The extent to which anyone can simply "be" in urban space tells us a lot about who has power, who feels their right to the city is a natural entitlement, and who will always be considered out of place. It reflects existing structures of discrimination in society and is therefore a good indicator of the remaining gaps between different groups. As a cisgender white woman, I'm highly unlikely to be asked to leave a public space, to have the police called on me, or to be followed through a department store. At the same time, however, I police my own clothing, posture, facial expressions, and other cues to avoid male harassment and unwanted attention. Rape culture teaches us that to be alone in public is to open yourself to the threat of sexual violence and thus vigilance is a part of the experience of being alone in the city for most women. But could it be otherwise? And how do we fight to make that happen?

CHAPTER 4 **CITY OF PROTEST**

I was arrested at one of my very first protests. I can't remember how I heard about the action, but it was probably through the Women's Centre at University of Toronto. I was in my second year of university, deep into my first women's studies courses, and dipping my toes into feminist organizations and activism on campus. A recently elected conservative provincial government was making severe cuts to services that would affect survivors of domestic violence and sexual assault. Women from anti-violence organizations like the Toronto Rape Crisis Centre wanted to shut down an intersection outside Queen's Park, the site of the Ontario legislature. I was ready to be directly involved in actions that would disrupt the city. I was ready to get arrested with my sisters.

There was a strong spirit of protest in Ontario in the mid- to late-1990s, as labour unions successfully organized massive one-day general strikes known as "Days of Action" beginning in late 1995. In what I believe was my first experience of a large scale protest, I went to the Toronto Day of Action on October 25, 1996. An estimated 250,000 people—the largest ever protest in

Ontario—marched five kilometres from the lakeshore up to the legislature.[175] It took all day for the end of the march to meet up with the beginning at Queen's Park. It was electrifying. I'd never felt part of something so big, so collectively energizing. I'd never experienced my city in that way before: taking over the streets, linking arms with strangers, expressing anger and joy and solidarity. I never wanted it to end.

So when we heard about the feminist activists organizing a direct action protest against the government's cuts to women's services, my friend and feminist mentor Theresa and I were eager to learn more. I felt a tingle up my spine every time I thought about it. I couldn't wait to take my feminist politics out of the classroom and into the street, coincidentally a mere block from where I was born. It felt right.

We met one night at the Women's Centre at U of T to prepare. The organizers wanted to make it really clear that this wasn't a sanctioned protest. We'd have no permits, no police protection. In fact, once the police arrived, we should expect to be arrested. The point of the meeting was to teach us, essentially, how to be dragged off the street by police safely and without risking a charge of resisting arrest.

In retrospect, it could only have been my youth, naiveté, and privilege that prevented me from understanding how truly audacious it was to plan to have fewer than thirty people block a major intersection in the middle of a weekday. I don't remember feeling scared, having second thoughts, or questioning the tactics of the organizers. I was excited to be included in this group of awe-inspiring activists who were ready to put themselves on the line for their beliefs. They prepared us well for what actually happened on the day of the protest. In fact, it all went down exactly as they'd predicted.

My most vivid mental images of the protest are of the giant white banner we carried, printed with the famous words of Black feminist scholar and activist Audre Lorde: "Your silence will not protect you."[176] We moved into the intersection en masse and sat down in a large ring. We chanted, but I don't remember what. I'm not sure how long it was before the police arrived. Officers began coming around, telling each of us to move or be arrested. No one got up. The organizers had warned us that the police might be rude, that they might taunt us. But none did. They were calm, and ultimately so were we, as one by one, we were each lifted off the ground from under our armpits by two officers. It was all very matter of fact. We were hoisted over to the police wagon, photographed, formally arrested, searched, and placed inside. We weren't handcuffed. Soon, the two-dozen or so protesters were loaded into vans, and before we knew it we'd travelled the short distance to 52 Division for an afternoon in the holding cell. The protest was over.

RIGHT TO THE CITY

Cities have been the primary sites of activism for most of the major social and political movements of the last two centuries. Combining a critical mass of people with the ability to take a message directly to the halls of power (governments, corporations, Wall Street, international organizations, etc.) and access to communications and media, cities offer the right mix of resources to make protest visible and effective. Even though social media has played an increasing role in generating momentum, for example through hashtags like #BlackLivesMatter, most movements still "take to the streets" at critical moments. Even if you've never participated in a protest, if you live in a city of any size, chances are high that you've witnessed some form of political action.

Activism, and public protest specifically, has connected me to cities and to my feminist politics in such critical ways. Long before I knew of the leftist urban concept of "the right to the city," participating in protests brought my sense of belonging in the city alive and confirmed my righteous indignation at the wide-spread injustices that affected not just my life, but the lives of millions of others. Protest events have always refueled that anger and my commitment to change in ways that keep me energized as a scholar and a teacher. They continue to teach me so much about concepts like solidarity and allyship, about feminism's relationship to other social movements, about intersectionality and its successes and failures. They animate everything I think about what a feminist city could and should be.

Images of fierce women taking to the streets of their cities easily fill my mind: suffragettes marching through Hyde Park; trans women of colour and drag queens on the frontlines against police at Stonewall in New York; the queer femme leaders of Black Lives Matter Toronto halting the 2016 Pride Parade; an estimated five million women across Kerala forming a human chain to fight for equal access to their temple. Throughout history, women have used the city as both the site and the stakes of struggle, as French Marxist philosopher Henri Lefebvre put it.[177] In other words, the city is the place to be heard; it's also the place we're fighting for. Fighting to belong, to be safe, to earn a living, to represent our communities, and so much more.[178]

Any attempt to sketch out a vision of the feminist city must consider the role of activism. Rarely, if ever, are marginalized groups "given" anything—freedom, rights, recognition, resources—without a struggle. Whether it's the right to vote, to ride the bus, or to enter spaces of power, people have always had to demand change. Sometimes that demand takes the form of public protest and feminist demands on the city are no different. I know that the freedoms I enjoy, while still incomplete, were generated by the bold actions of the "many-gendered mothers," to borrow a phrase from Maggie Nelson, who fought with their minds and hearts and bodies to claim some access to the city and all that it entails: work, education, culture, politics, and more. Recalling this history and finding my own place in it are central to my thinking about feminist cities of the present and the future. Nothing that we have wasn't fought for; nothing that we'll gain in the future will be given without a fight.

Women's urban activism takes many forms. In the late nineteenth century, women like Jane Addams and Ida B. Wells in Chicago not only advocated for women, especially immigrant and Black women, they pioneered new residential and educational models like Hull House and new ways of studying and understanding women's urban lives. In the late twentieth century, women planners engaged in municipal activism to get gender issues on the urban agenda, for example through the work of groups like Women Plan Toronto.[179] Even the "toilet ladies" that we encountered in the previous chapter are part of the long and impressive history of this activism. I want to think more specifically about activism that takes the form of collective protest, using the physical space of the city to take on the powerful forces—governments, corporations, employers, the police, etc.— that shape the lives of women and other marginalized people. Protests are never without their own internal struggles and contradictions, all of which have pushed me to consider anew what feminism is and what feminist spaces look like.[180]

My first Take Back the Night (TBTN) march happened shortly after the Queen's Park protest. I saw so many familiar faces, including women from the anti-violence protest, the Toronto Rape Crisis

Centre, and the U of T Women's Centre. With candles, hot chocolate, and increasingly hoarse voices, the women-only march made its way from downtown towards the east end. With the early gentrification of many west end neighbourhoods, Toronto just east of Yonge Street was the place where many poor, working class, and homeless people had been pushed. Stigmatized as a high-crime area, this was also a place where street-based sex work was still visible. In other words, the east side of downtown was a place that existed as a fearful, degenerate zone in the public imagination. It was a place deemed scary and dangerous for women.

TBTN marches date back to the mid-1970s in North America, when radical feminists in cities such as Philadelphia, New York, and San Francisco held protests to raise awareness about violence against women. TBTN isn't only about reclaiming nighttime, but also about space: it insists that women have the right to access all city spaces, at any time, safely and confidently. In Canada, Vancouver was the first city to set up a regular march under the organization of Vancouver Rape Relief. Sexual assault crisis centres across the country started to plan annual marches for the third Friday of September in order to coordinate national efforts.[181] Many cities, small and large (even tiny Sackville), all over the world, hold TBTN events on a regular basis or in response to particularly troubling acts of violence against women in public spaces.

As a west end girl myself, I was mostly unfamiliar with anything east of the gay village on Church Street. Venturing east with the march was exhilarating. I'd never have wandered over there by myself. Because the area was unfamiliar to me at the time, I don't remember exactly where we went. I do recall pausing outside of one of Toronto's iconic strip clubs. It was probably Jilly's (now a boutique hotel) at Queen and Broadview. It didn't occur to me at the time to question whether this was exclusionary toward sex workers, or whether sex workers were part of the imagined group of women for whom we were "taking back" the night. I was a little too green and too unabashedly excited to be fully conscious of the broader politics shaping TBTN in the 1990s. The so-called "sex wars" in feminism between anti-pornography/anti-violence activists like Andrea Dworkin and Catherine MacKinnon and "pro-sex" third wave feminists were in full effect. For some, TBTN was a prime example of the anti-sex politics of feminism and its inability to reckon with the agency of women involved in sex work including prostitution, erotic dancing, and pornography. Indeed, a well-known anti-pornography text from 1980 had the title *Take Back the Night: Women and Pornography*.[182] Unfortunately, none of this troubled me as we stopped to make a racket outside of Jilly's.

I also wasn't thinking about the politics of the event as a women-only space. Sure, my women's studies classes had covered the difficulties in defining "woman" and the groups historically excluded from the category, but to be honest we didn't talk much about trans women, and gender fluidity and non-binary identities were rarely considered. For me as a cis woman (a concept definitely not in use in the mid-1990s!) the "women-only" character of TBTN was part of the excitement and the feeling of empowerment. I didn't stop to think about whether trans women would be welcomed, just as I hadn't thought about the sex workers whose jobs we were potentially interrupting with our shouting, nor about the women who lived in these neighbourhoods and how they felt about this act of "taking back."

With perspective, age, and more exposure to critiques from Black and Indigenous people, people of colour, disabled people, and trans folks, I have a better appreciation for how protest spaces can and do reproduce systems of privilege and oppression, as well as violent practices. Now I know enough to cringe over the colonial attitude implicit in the action of "taking back" and about the race and class dynamics of directing the march through the east side of downtown. Given the radical feminist roots of the TBTN movement and the hostility that some self-proclaimed radical feminists have towards trans women, I imagine that these marches were not experienced as safe and welcoming spaces for trans women. Although trans women are disproportionately victims of gender-based violence, they've had to create their own spaces of activism while also fighting for inclusion into feminist events and spaces.[183] Recently, the adoption of the pink "pussy hat" symbol for the anti-Trump Women's Marches was flagged as an example of how narrow biological understandings of womanhood can still infiltrate feminist organizing, symbolically excluding trans, intersex, and non-binary people.

Marches and protests also implicitly normalize able-bodiedness, with their emphasis on motion, the ability to take over any space, and the possibility of physical confrontation. Although disabled people have been engaging in highly visible and even confrontational protests around disability rights for decades, including recent occupations of U.S. Senate offices over changes to the Americans With Disabilities Act, most protests not focused on disability fail miserably at accessibility. From inaccessible routes and gathering places, the speed of movement, and a lack of accommodations for different visual and auditory needs, to the use of ableist language in chants and placards, urban protests have typically excluded disabled people.

Evidence of the work of disabled people and trans people in encouraging activist organizations to do better is apparent. TBTN in cities like Toronto is now explicitly intersectional in its aims and organizing. Its website describes TBTN as a grassroots event that honours the experiences of survivors of sexual violence; sexual assault, childhood sexual violence, domestic violence and survivors of state violence such as police brutality, racism, sexist oppression and other forms of institutionalized violence.... The event is welcome to all genders and is trans inclusive.[184]

The event also ensures wheelchair accessibility, ASL interpretation, attendant care, and childcare.

DIY SAFETY

In the early 1990s, though, TBTN was more concerned with responding to the terror many women were experiencing in their city's streets. In Toronto, the years of horrific attacks and eventually abductions and murders committed by "Scarborough rapist" Paul Bernardo were just coming to an end. The memory of the "balcony rapist" Paul Callow, who raped five women on the east side near Wellesley and Sherbourne in the mid-1980s after gaining access to their apartments via ground level balconies, was still fresh. His fifth victim, known as "Jane Doe," had brought a lawsuit against Toronto police for their deliberate decision not to warn women about the string of attacks; in effect, police were using women as bait in order to catch the rapist.[185] Jane Doe won her case in 1998, but the ongoing saga reminded many of us that the police weren't reliable allies in stopping violence against women. A "taking matters into our own hands approach" was deemed necessary. In this context, TBTN marches made a point to visit parts of the city where women had faced public violence and where they couldn't rely on police protection.

Women's anti-violence actions in the city take place in a world where the police are seen as indifferent bystanders at best.

Infamously, Vancouver police and the RCMP long refused to connect the multiple disappearances of women from the Downtown Eastside—many of whom were Indigenous and/or sex workers—to the possible activities of a serial killer. Reviews of the force's actions and attitudes in light of the discovery and eventual conviction of a man for six murders (although he is said to have confessed to almost fifty) revealed outright racism and sexism among the police and their staff, as well as a deep disrespect for sex workers. The *Red Women Rising* report, prepared by the Downtown Eastside Women's Centre, highlights women's ongoing mistrust of the police:

> In the DTES, the criminalization of poverty overlapping with the specific over-surveillance and over-policing of Indigenous women marks the beginning of lengthy entanglements with the criminal justice system through the courts and prisons. Fundamentally, the criminal justice system is an inappropriate and oppressive tool to resolve social and economic issues, and the Canadian legal system is a foreign and colonial system imposed upon Indigenous peoples.

The report's recommendations include increased accountability for the police, the end of street checks, and the repealing of laws that criminalize or increase harm for women in the sex trade. Women in the Downtown Eastside have held a memorial march on February 14th every year since 1992 to honour the lives of missing and murdered women and all women's lives lost in the area.[186]

The Slutwalks protests, created in 2011, are among those actions directly sparked by police attitudes. At a campus safety information session at York University's Osgoode Hall law school, a Toronto police officer told the attendees that a woman shouldn't "dress like a slut" if she wished to remain safe from assault.[187] Outraged, women and allies organized a series of marches called Slutwalks in cities across Canada and eventually around the world. The Slutwalks took place on city streets and university campuses. Participants deliberately challenged the idea that victims of sexual assault are "asking for it" by the way they dress by wearing all sorts of outrageous outfits, "slutty" and otherwise. They remind the public that rape culture is pervasive, and that the police have usually done more to uphold rape culture than to challenge it.[188]

Although women in other cities sometimes removed the name "Slutwalks" and encouraged women to dress normally, the message about the need to challenge the normalization of harassment and violence remained similar. Women's and gender studies scholar Durba Mitra reflected on Slutwalks-inspired actions across India in 2011, noting that the "Pride Stride" events, or in Hindi, *Besharmi Morcha* ("Shameless Rally"), garnered intense opposition from the police. While events in Bhopal and Delhi proceeded, a Bangalore protest was cancelled. Mitra shows that the police actively participate in victim blaming, citing a director of police who "blamed women for provoking men with 'fashionable clothing'."[189] Although the Pride Strides in India didn't draw the same kinds of numbers as events in cities like Toronto, in part because of the lack of purchase of western feminist attempts to reclaim terms and concepts like "slut," Mitra claims that they nonetheless contributed to an important conversation about social regulation of women and the normalization of violence.

While the #MeToo movement has been largely associated with an online presence and high-profile survivors telling their stories, women across the world have seized this moment to heighten their mobilizations against harassment and gendered violence and to protest the failures of the police, criminal justice systems, and other institutions to counter violence. The hashtag #Cuéntalo ("tell your story") emerged in response to the acquittal of five men on rape charges in Pamplona in June 2018, spreading to Latin America and galvanizing women to respond to high rates of femicide and perceived impunity for perpetrators. In Chile, students "launched a wave of strikes, occupations and protests against sexual harassment and sexual discrimination within the country's universities" in spring and summer 2018. Connecting their cause to the wider issues of violence and lack of reproductive rights across the region, the student activists immobilized the higher education system and promised that this was the beginning of a wider movement into other sectors of society.[190]

All of these movements push back against the "naturalized" geographies of rape culture: the idea that sexual assault is almost inevitable in certain spaces (university campuses, "bad" neighbourhoods) and that "vulnerable" people like women must either avoid those places or take precautions such as dressing conservatively. In the 1990s, as I came into adulthood, events like TBTN helped me confirm that what I felt—a ball of righteous fury at a million double standards—was valid. It wasn't just my still-developing teenage brain being angry at the world. It was a legitimate reaction to a system. A system that made different rules for me as a young woman in the city. A system that threatened to punish me with sexual violence if I disobeyed those rules. Marches and protests taught me that it was okay, and good, and necessary to push back. They gave me an outlet to express and articulate my early feminist claims to the city. They also pushed me to think about how my privileges make certain kinds of actions, emotions, and even the reclaiming of slurs like "slut" available to me but not so much for others. In other words, I was learning that feminist politics in the city were fraught with entangled power relations.

GENDERED ACTIVIST LABOUR

These early experiences should have prepared me well to recognize the power dynamics and hierarchies that pervade other movements. Yet I admit I was caught off guard by the sexism, racism, ableism, and transphobia that I witnessed in other spaces, especially spaces of labour activism. Going on strike made these fissures extremely obvious. In 2008, I'd just finished my PhD at York University but was still a unionized part-time instructor. Our union went on strike in early November and we were out until the end of January. Three months of standing in the cold at key intersections surrounding campus, slowing down traffic, and stopping most university operations. It was stressful and dangerous work, blocking traffic in a city where people feel their right to drive is practically enshrined in the Charter. It wasn't long before entrenched heteronormative assumptions about activism, care, and gendered divisions of labour started to show up on the picket lines.

Suddenly my bookish and soft-spoken male colleagues were channeling an inner "man of the woods," chopping down trees for the fire barrels and showing off their fire-making skills. Confrontations with vehicles and drivers escalated quickly as men rushed angrily toward any prickly situation. Meanwhile, women and queer folks were quietly taking on the emotional and domestic labour. We came in to calm down angry drivers, comfort rattled or injured strikers, make more hot chocolate, and keep the mood elevated with music and dance. By the time we noticed these dynamics, everyone had settled into their "strike roles," and it was hard to challenge the patterns that were established. It was the traditional hetero-patriarchal family come to life at an urban intersection.

I knew intellectually that social movements were often gendered in this way. Men become the charismatic, visionary, public leaders. They appear to chart the course of the movement and make major decisions for all involved. Women leaders are often written out of official accounts or ignored by the media. In recalling the nineteen-month occupation of Alcatraz Island by members of the American Indian Movement in 1969, LaNada War Jack notes that men were credited with "taking Alcatraz" while women's leadership was underplayed.[191] Women are often found doing the on-the-ground, physical, emotional, and domestic labour. Women go door-to-door to raise awareness, they print the flyers, they make the sandwiches, they get the permits, they write the press releases. At Alcatraz, women set up the kitchen, school, and medical facilities that sustained the lengthy occupation, vital after most resources were cut off by the Coast Guard. Women care for the emotions of others and sustain the relationships between members of the movement.[192] Occupy Edmonton activist Chelsea Taylor described the habits of men at their 2011 Occupy camp: "narcissistic posturing, poor listening, an aversion to menial tasks."[193] Even more disheartening: women often face danger from fellow activists. Sexual harassment and abuse is an open secret in many movements, but women are often encouraged to keep silent for the sake of the cause.[194]

Up at York, these dynamics came to a head when strikers with disabilities, chronic illness, or child care issues who performed their strike work in the main office pointed out that their contributions weren't recognized or valued by those on the eight outdoor picket lines. Even though the administrative and organizational work was absolutely foundational, it wasn't the gritty, dangerous, cold work of the picket line. It was domestic, warm, and safe: in other words, feminized. Dubbing themselves the "Ninth Line," the administrative strikers pushed the rest of the union to value their labour and recognize the sexist and ableist patterns behind the differential valuing of strike actions.

The unspoken assumptions behind ideas about who protesters and strikers are were also becoming clear as I tried to juggle activism and parenting. Some of Maddy's earliest experiences of big marches were Pride parades, which by the early 2000s were primarily celebratory events rather than spaces of protest. Grad school friends and I would also bundle up the kids and break out the strollers every March for International Women's Day. Typically, the day began with a rally on the University of Toronto campus and continued with a march through downtown toward city hall. The kids were amazing troopers. Early March is still cold and let's be honest, the rally held little of interest for kids aged two to six. But perhaps these chilly marches prepared Maddy to come with me to rallies at Queen's Park during the York strike. She loved it, even in the January cold. I think she's always had an anarchist spirit. She was right in her element, yelling at political representatives, staring down police. But in many cases, parenting responsibilities don't mix well with protests and activism.

In June 2010, the G20 meetings were held in Toronto, with G8 meetings just north of the city in Huntsville. The city had already been in an ultra-securitized state for weeks, with walls going up around meeting sites and controversial emergency laws giving police a set of otherwise illegal powers. It was the summer after my first year in Sackville and I was back home for a few months before getting ready to move full-time to New Brunswick. The G20 protest wasn't an event I was about to miss. The Toronto summit was scheduled for the weekend of June 26–27, but the week before saw a series of increasingly big marches building up to the massive protests. On Friday the 25th, I made my way down to the park at Allan Gardens. I joined thousands of people getting ready to march toward Toronto police headquarters, led by the immigrant rights group No One is Illegal. Heading into the park, I was illegally searched by police but I wanted to make it to the march so I held my tongue while he rummaged through my bag. The scarf I planned to use as a tear gas mask was wrapped prettily around my hair, so at least he wouldn't confiscate that.

As the crowd eventually made its way into the street, police lined both sides of the crowd, using their bikes as barricades. Although they were still dressed in normal summer uniforms, riot masks were hanging from their handlebars. The march began slowly, heading west. I wasn't far from the front when we paused outside of police headquarters. A few blocks back, something was happening. The police had rushed in on some protesters. There was now a gap in the group and people were scrambling backwards to see what was happening. "Paper Planes" by M.I.A. was blasting from a portable sound system. I can't forget the suddenly wide-eyed look of a police officer as she realized that the signal to get into riot masks and other gear had been given. She fumbled anxiously to pull the mask off her handlebars and get it in place as the police assumed a more aggressive stance. Things were heating up.

This was a day before the infamous kettling incident and mass arrests that were to come on Saturday and Sunday. On June 27th, police circled and contained over three hundred people (some protesters, some just walking by) at Queen Street and Spadina Avenue for four hours in the pouring rain in a tactic known as kettling. Hundreds were arrested, bringing the total to an aston-ishing eleven hundred people over the course of the weekend.[195] Protesters were detained in completely inadequate facilities with little food, no medical attention, and no communications. Eventually, even more heinous elements of the detention event were uncovered, including the sexual harassment and assault of women and non-binary people.[196] At the Friday march, we had no idea how bad it was about to get between police and protesters. On Friday, things seemed "normal." Police did make some arrests, but they were minimal compared to what was coming. I'd been arrested before and wasn't unwilling to let it happen again. One thing was different though. My ten-year old daughter was at day care and waiting for me to pick her up.

As the march continued west, nearing Queen's Park and the subway station before it would turn toward downtown, I had to make a quick decision. Continue to walk and participate in the heart of the protest as it approached the highly securitized zone near the summit where things were sure to get riskier, or scamper out of formation and duck into the subway, ensuring I could make it back to the west end in time for day care pick up. I remember feeling a hot flush of anger as I realized this was a choice women throughout history have had to make: be politically active, with all of its risks, or perform your duties as a caregiver in the private, depoliticized space of the home. Not only is this a systemic way that women are excluded from opportunities to have their voices heard by the state, but women's disproportionate responsibility for child care is typically ignored by protest organizers as well.

When the march began to turn the corner, my partner and I had a quick conversation: Who would stay and who would go? Feeling the tug of responsibility, I decided I would be the one to leave. The anger I felt was joined by shame as I broke ranks and hustled towards the subway entrance. I felt like I was abandoning my comrades at a critical moment. It was embarrassing to think that others might believe I was running off because I was scared or simply not committed. As I sat down in the subway car, surrounded by strangers who didn't know or care about my politics, I shifted from a radical demonstrator to just another mom heading out to pick up her kid from day care. It seemed that the two identities couldn't be joined together.

In the aftermath of the G20 protests, when the full extent of the police force's actions against the people of Toronto came to light, more demonstrations were held. On Canada Day, I went to Queen's Park, this time with Maddy, to take part in a pro-democracy rally and march. Surrounded by friends and draped in a rainbow peace flag, Maddy got her first real taste of a massive demonstration on the streets of her city. I remember chanting "this is what democracy looks like!" over and over as we marched. Maddy was old enough to understand what was happening but not experienced enough to get why the police had acted as they had. "Didn't they have rules they were supposed to follow?" "Yes, but...". "Didn't people have a right to protest?" "Yes, but..." During those days following the G20, she started to understand that living in a democracy means you have to actively exercise your rights. And sometimes that means you have to take to the streets to remind those in power of their responsibilities and obligations. It didn't surprise me at all when, eight years later, I got a video of Maddy from the frontlines of a #MeToo rally at McGill University.

Women have balanced motherhood and political activism by bringing our kids when we can, but we face censure for doing so and always worry about our kids' safety. People will ask, "Aren't you putting your kids in danger?" "Aren't you indoctrinating them with your beliefs rather than letting them make up their own minds?" The strict lines between politics and motherhood extend well beyond activist circles. Women made international headlines in 2018 just for being pregnant while in office. New Zealand Prime Minister Jacinda Ardern is one of the very few female heads of state ever to become pregnant in office. She had to declare to the obsessed press: "I'm pregnant, not incapacitated" to justify continuing her duties as normal.[197] One day after the U.S. Senate changed the rules to allow babies onto the floor during votes, Senator Tammy Duckworth became the first to cast a vote with her newborn at her side.[198] And in Canada, Karina Gould became the first federal cabinet minister to have a baby while in office.[199] The fact that these "firsts" are happening almost two decades into the twenty-first century is mind boggling. For professional politicians, motherhood and especially the obvious sights of pregnancy, breastfeeding, babies, and children are seen as incommensurable with political activities. For those who take the activist route, we still have to second guess ourselves both as mothers and as activists—are we appropriately committed to both? Is that even possible?

ACTIVIST TOURISM

Motherhood certainly changed my relationship to protesting in terms of how I could and would act on the ground, but overall it only strengthened my commitments. It was important to me to teach my daughter the importance of public demonstration. Even in Sackville, we kept this spirit alive as often as we could. In some ways, small town events are even more significant, as events like Pride parades and TBTN marches are often relatively new to small rural communities.

Still, the chance to participate in protests is one of the things I miss most about living in a city, but once in a while I stumble across a demonstration while I'm travelling. A few years ago, I decided to skip a few conference sessions while in New York City. A friend suggested I check out St. Marks Bookshop (now closed) in the East Village. At the checkout counter, I spotted a small flyer for an Occupy Town Square event in Tompkins Square Park, happening that very day. It seemed fortuitous: I'd always wanted to see Tompkins Square, the scene of radical anti-gentrification protests a couple of decades earlier. I'd read about the park so many times in classic writing on gentrification, but never had the chance to visit. I paid for my books and set off along Avenue A towards East 7th and the park.

This was February 2012, about six months after the Occupy Wall Street protest kicked off in September 2011. Occupy Town Square events were popping up all over, providing alternative temporary encampment sites and spreading the Occupy message to neighbourhoods across major cities. In Tompkins Square Park, the one-day event somehow looked as though it had always been there. There was a kitchen, a library, a knitting circle, drummers, stilt walkers, artists, T-shirt making, and, standing watchfully by, a disproportionate number of police officers observing the completely chill and peaceful gathering. I stopped to talk to David, an artist experiencing homelessness who was exchanging clever cardboard signs for donations. I picked one up that read "Honey I'm cold, can we go occupy a Starbucks now?" As I wandered from group to group, sometimes chatting with folks, sometimes just looking, I finally felt connected—in a very small way—to the Occupy movement.

As the afternoon edged towards evening, demonstrators began to gather together for a more vocal protest to end the day. A megaphone appeared and a small crowd formed along the pathway. The police were suddenly on alert. They moved closer together and closer to the demonstrators. The atmosphere was still quite calm and I didn't sense that confrontation was likely. I hovered near the edges of the gathered demonstrators, until it occurred to me that I wasn't at home. I'm not an American citizen. I didn't have my passport. A comfortable bubble of Canadian innocence and my privilege as a white woman had allowed me to ignore my less-solid position at a New York protest. Many others never have the luxury of forgetting that police or other agents of the state can target them at any time. In most cases, I can use that privilege to take part in demonstrations on behalf of others who have less safety. But I didn't want to find out what would happen if I was approached by police or even arrested at an Occupy protest, with no ID beyond my conference badge and maybe my New Brunswick driver's license. Regretfully, I backed away from the group and made my way to the subway, returning to the bland safety of midtown and the convention centre.

I wanted to see Tompkins Square Park because of its history as a site of struggle for the right to the city among poor, working class, and immigrant communities facing displacement by gentrification. It was amazing to find that Tompkins Square was still a place where activists gathered, even for short periods of time. While the neighbourhood itself is gentrified, the significance of Tompkins Square as a historical site of urban activism remained salient.

Some places just seem to have a spirit of resistance built right into them, where long histories of protest have saturated communities even as the demographics of those communities have changed. This was how Chicago's Lower West Side was described to me when I visited the neighbourhoods of Pilsen and Little Village to do research on environmental justice activism and resistance to gentrification. Chicago's west side was the birthplace of radical labour activism in the U.S., with events like the Haymarket Riots, Battle of Halsted Street Viaduct, garment strikes, women's strikes, and more rocking Chicago in the late nineteenth and early twentieth centuries. Immigrant labourers on the west side—first eastern Europeans and then, by the mid-twentieth century, Mexicans—struggled for their rights to safe working conditions and fair pay.[200] At the same time, they had to fight for their homes and neighbourhoods, as massive urban renewal projects displaced thousands and pushed them further west into the areas that now comprise the "Mexico of the Midwest."

By the time I was getting to know Pilsen and Little Village in 2015, the predominantly Latinx communities were fighting new battles against environmental racism and the gradual onslaught of gentrification as high real estate prices in other areas drove young white folks west in search of lower rents. Pilsen and Little Village had long been home to a variety of industries, toxic lands, waterways, and ongoing sources of pollution such as coal-fired power plants. Environmental justice organizers in Little Village and community organizers in Pilsen drew on the long histories of political activism in these neighbourhoods, histories that predated the arrival of Mexican and other Latinx immigrants. Protest was in the bones of the Lower West Side, they said. Combined with the specific experiences of Mexican and other Latinx migrants fighting displacement, racism, and xenophobic immigration policies, a powerful brand of resistance was fostered and sustained here.[201]

I saw signs of this all over the communities. From the massive, vibrant murals depicting culturally-significant events and local heroes to the hastily scrawled anti-gentrification slogans ("Pilsen is not for sale!/*Pilsen no se vende!*"), there was a palpable sense of commitment to an ongoing struggle against forces seeking to remove and further marginalize their communities. I don't want to romanticize these struggles or the neighbourhoods themselves, but I believed the activists who felt that resistance was not only in their blood, but also in the bricks and mortar of their communities.

At the same time, I was very aware that this history of resistance was being diminished (even co-opted in some cases) by the influx of white, middle-class renters, homeowners, and businesses, especially in Pilsen, which had already been gentrifying for many years. I was also aware that I was part of the problem. A white researcher, renting Airbnb apartments at inflated prices, my presence confirming the normalcy of white hipsters in a long-time Latinx community. Yes, I was there to study and hopefully support the efforts of community organizations to resist displacement. But I was also contributing to gentrification through my very presence and perhaps undermining the movements I wanted to learn more about.

PROTEST LESSONS

Over my many years as a student, activist, teacher, and researcher, I've been taught many lessons about the tensions and even contradictions of feminist and urban activism. I didn't know anything about protest back when I volunteered to get arrested at the anti-violence protest. I thought simply "being a feminist" was solidarity enough. It wasn't until after the arrest that I truly understood how deep divisions can run through movements. The twenty or so of us who were arrested and charged with mischief wanted to meet to discuss our next steps. Theresa and I had a large space available in the common room of our U of T residence. To us, it was a dated and slightly shabby room, with a smelly carpet and sprung furniture. But to some of the more seasoned activists, the ornate stone building with its giant fireplaces and hardwood floors reeked of privilege. They weren't wrong. I just hadn't been able to see it that way before. Theresa and I suddenly knew we weren't fully trusted anymore.

These and other divisions across age, class, and race made for tense negotiations. Some argued that since the justice system was itself classist, racist, and patriarchal, we should refuse to engage to the maximum possible extent. Others were still minors who now had to consider their parents' wishes. Others wanted to deal with the charges with the least amount of energy possible in order to make time for the next effort. All of these positions were reasonable, but they led to a shockingly quick breakdown in the mutual pride and solidarity we felt while planning and executing the protest. It was the first time I realized that being a women's studies student might actually make other feminists distrust me, rather than see me as an obvious ally with the same commitments to social change. It had never occurred to me that my education would be anything but an asset in feminist social movements. I was shaken, but I was being schooled in intersectionality.

The city of Toronto was given a big old intersectional wake-up call in 2016 when Black Lives Matter Toronto (BLM-TO) brought the massive Pride Parade to a grinding halt for thirty minutes. BLM is one of the fiercest examples of intersectional urban movement organizing going. Started by three women in the wake of the murder of Trayvon Martin, BLM recognizes the deep interconnections among issues like gendered housing insecurity, gentrification, domestic violence, poverty, racism, and police brutality. BLM chapters in the U.S. as well as Canada are at the forefront of pushing cities to both reckon with their discriminatory legacies and to imagine different urban futures. On a sweltering July Sunday in Toronto, BLM-TO presented Pride Toronto with a list of demands that, as Black queer scholar and activist Rinaldo Walcott put it, plunged "Toronto's queer community into a Queer Civil War," one that would shake "Toronto the good's" love affair with Pride for years to come.[202]

I just happened to be in Toronto that weekend and decided to take in the parade. We'd already caught sight of Prime Minister Justin Trudeau hopping into a black SUV on his way to the marshaling area, pink shirt and all. The sun was shining and energy was high as the first floats turned onto Yonge Street, dance music thumping, abs rippling, water guns squirting. Indigenous drummers and BLM-TO were at the head of the parade. Trudeau followed soon after to a great round of cheers. I remember commenting to my partner that the police marching in uniform were my least favourite part of Pride. I'd cringe as the crowd exploded in support for these armed officers. But before that could even happen this year, the parade stopped. We weren't seeing anything but the huge corporate float paused in front of us. It wasn't until later that we realized what had happened a few blocks south. Encircled by Indigenous drummers, BLM-TO activists sat down in the intersection of Yonge and College, refusing to budge until the head of Pride agreed to their list of demands. The one that would become the most controversial: "a ban on police forces marching in uniform or full regalia and carrying guns at the parade."[203]

For the Black queer activists leading BLM-TO, an understanding of how the police continued to criminalize and target queer of colour and Indigenous youth, sex workers, trans people, and queer people living in poverty was central to their claim that Pride was a corporate, white-washed space, one that ignored the ongoing marginalization of the most vulnerable members of the community in return for mainstream support from the city, corporations, and organizations like the police and military. Walcott, who participated in the sit-down, notes:

> The co-ordination between BLM-TO and the Indigenous community signaled a different relationship to contemporary politics. It signaled that Black and Indigenous activists and thinkers are seeking ways to work together.... It would be insincere to believe that those impacted by the brutalities of policing are not Black queer and Indigenous Two-Spirit peoples, because they are.[204]

Calling for a ban on police in uniform highlighted a disconnect in the queer community. Many in the mainstream queer community see Pride as a time of pure celebration and believe that police marching in the parade represents progress, inclusion, and acceptance. BLM-TO and their supporters argue that policing represents a "clear and present danger for them" and that a failure to recognize this is a failure to include Black and Indigenous people, people of colour, trans people, sex workers, and poor people in Pride. It's also part of the slow erasure of the roots of Pride in anti-police riots, starting with New York's Stonewall Inn riots in 1969 and with Toronto's riots in response to bathhouse raids in 1981. The BLM-TO intervention initiated a wave of change. Although the board of Pride tried to reinstate the police for the 2019 parade, the membership of the organization voted this proposal down, suggesting that many have received and even welcomed the message of BLM-TO.

It's been over twenty years since the protest where I was arrested. Like all activists and politically-committed scholars I've had to learn the hard way (which is the only way, really) that you'll encounter more contradictions than resolutions in your work, especially when your privileges become salient. As I moved from being a student to a full-time academic, my commitment to the intersection of feminist politics and right to the city movements has had to find new modes of expression. I get to stand in front of a classroom and initiate conversations about police violence, sexual harassment, rape culture, LGBTQ2S+ spaces, ableism, settler colonialism, and dozens of other politically-charged topics. I try to cultivate and support student activism at every opportunity. I'm committed to union solidarity. But I'd be the first to say that sometimes you just need to be a body out in the streets. Rights aren't won and defended in a classroom, on social media, or even via electoral politics. The work has to happen on the ground.

History is clear that social change doesn't happen without some form of protest, and indeed most of the improvements in women's lives in cities can be traced back to activist movements. Not every woman will participate in some form of protest; in fact, most never will. But all of our lives have been shaped by them. For me, activist spaces are my greatest teachers. I wouldn't be able to articulate what a feminist city aspires to without those experiences. I've learned a lot about how to protest over the years, but more importantly, I've learned that a feminist city is one you have to be willing to fight for.

CHAPTER 5: **CITY OF FEAR**

I was born in 1975, perfect timing for a childhood haunted by the spectre of stranger danger. At school, we had yearly visits from police officers demonstrating the latest techniques for avoiding kidnappers. Never tell a caller you're home alone. Have a code word that only you and your parents know. Never help anyone search for a lost puppy. Don't accept candy. With the rise of the international 24-hour news cycle, tales of missing children captured our wide-eyed attention and reminded us to be ever so cautious. The 1985 disappearance of eight-year-old Nicole Morin in Toronto's west end, not far from where we lived, was a scary moment. I was almost ten. Nicole got into the elevator on the way to her building's pool and vanished without a trace. Her picture was everywhere: a normal looking kid with mousy brown hair like mine. More than thirty years later, she's never been found. The image of a little girl in a red striped bathing suit disappearing in mere moments is still a haunting one.

It probably wasn't long after Nicole Morin's presumed kidnapping that the general threat of stranger danger started to take on a particularly gendered shape for me. The generic kidnapper slowly gained the more specific features of a predator who targets girls and women. I became conscious of being vulnerable not just because I was a child, but because I was a girl. There was no one moment or lesson that delivered this message. Rather, it was a gradual layering of subtle cues that, when condensed, sent a clear signal about where danger resided, and how I was to avoid it.

We lived in a townhouse in a working class suburban neighbourhood when I was a kid. There were lots of families around, but our nearest neighbours were boys a few years older than my brother and I. The first couple of years we all played together with no concerns: baseball in the hydro field, hockey in the driveway, riding our Big Wheels up and down the street. As the years passed, the boys became teenagers while my brother and I remained kids. Strangely, my parents became wary of those boys, especially if my girlfriends and I went out to play. It was nothing explicit. Just a sense that something had shifted and we should "be careful." One afternoon the boys pretended to kidnap my friend and I by corralling us behind the hockey net in their garage, saying they weren't going to let us leave. Of course, they did, but the joke felt a little sinister in a way our childhood games hadn't. Suddenly it seemed like maybe my mom was right to worry. About what, I was still a little unclear.

Late night bunk bed chatter at summer camp continued my education. Whenever we talked about boys the stories were tinged with a sense of danger. The clichéd summer camp "panty raids" were the kinds of things we could speak openly about, but we knew there was more to the danger of boys than underwear theft. No one wanted to name the threat of rape or molestation. We knew that being alone and going out at night were the times when those threats might become real. We were starting to understand that we were never supposed to be alone around boys and that we needed to always have a plan for our own safety.

There's no way I can do justice to the puberty years and describe all the messages girls receive about our bodies, clothing, hair, makeup, weight, hygiene, and behaviour that feed into the bigger message about controlling ourselves for the sake of safety. This is when the volume turns up on the message that girls and women are vulnerable due to our gender and that sexual development is going to make that danger real. Instructions about appropriate behavior (how you sit, speak, walk, hold yourself, etc.) take on a sense of urgency that indicates they're not just about polite social behaviour. Some women can pinpoint the exact moment they became aware that something was different. Maybe it was the day mom told you to start cinching your robe around your nightdress, or the night when your playful use of mom's makeup and high heels went from cute to inappropriate. For many of us, however, the message comes in like an IV drip, building up in our systems so gradually that once we become aware of it, it's fully dissolved in the bloodstream. It's already natural, common sense, inherent.

THE FEMALE FEAR
The socialization is so powerful and so deep that "female fear" itself has been assumed to be an innate trait of girls and women. The ubiquity of "female fear" has fascinated psychologists, criminologists, sociologists, and others who want to understand human behaviour. When I started doing research for my master's project on women's feelings of safety and fear in urban and suburban spaces, the volume of research seeking to explain women's fear overwhelmed me. From evolutionary biology to anthropology to women's and gender studies, there are few disciplines that

haven't weighed in on the topic.[205] Surveys on fear of crime and fear of violence were popular with social scientists in the 1980s and 1990s for gathering data about where, when, and with whom women experience fear. Study after study produced similar patterns: women identified cities, night-time, and strangers as primary sources of threat. In Canadian and American studies from the early 1990s, women's reported rate of fear was up to three times the reported rate of men's fear.[206]

By this time, enough data had been gathered on domestic violence and crimes against women in general for social scientists to know that women are much more likely to experience violence at the hands of people known to them, in private spaces such as home and workplaces. Men were more likely to be victims of (reported) crimes in public spaces, such as assault or mugging. Yet women consistently recount being fearful of strangers in public spaces. This seeming disconnect was labeled the "paradox of women's fear," with some researchers characterizing women's feelings as "irrational" and "unexplained" by the evidence. As Carolyn Whitzman notes, the refrain was, "What's wrong with these women anyhow?"[207] Of course, these studies didn't ask if people felt safe in their homes. Fear of crime has always been assumed to be a public phenomenon, an assumption that itself suggests a lack of gendered analysis from the outset.

Feminist geographers, sociologists, and psychologists were, shockingly, not happy with the conclusion that women are irrational. Not only did this reinforce a tired stereotype, it was probably bad science. If your best explanation is that the feelings and behaviour of a huge group of people are irrational, you're likely not digging deep enough into the phenomenon. A wider analysis of socialization, power, heteropatriarchy, and trauma revealed that the so-called paradox of women's fear was only paradoxical when viewed through a lens that ignored gendered power relations.[208] From a feminist perspective that takes women's lived realities seriously, the paradox was nothing of the kind, nor were women remotely irrational. Whitzman insists that those puzzled over women's fear were ignoring some essential—and for feminists, somewhat obvious—facts. At the top of her list: "The crime women most fear is rape. The crime men most fear is robbery. Robbery is a bad thing to have happen to you. Rape is worse."[209]

That sexual violence generates a heightened sense of fear seems clear, but this factor was hidden by the generic nature of fear of crime surveys. Feminist scholars also point out that sexual assault is grossly underreported, suggesting that rates of violence against women are massively underestimated using statistics based on reported crimes. The experience of prior assault is also likely to leave women with an intensified fear of future assault. The very everyday experiences of catcalling and sexual harassment serve to reinforce fear as women are constantly sexualized, objectified, and made to feel uncomfortable in public spaces.[210] Geographer Hille Koskela observes that "sexual harassment reminds women every day that they are not meant to be in certain spaces."[211]

The long-term effect of childhood socialization has to be considered as well. We're given very explicit instructions to fear strangers and public spaces at night. The news media also plays a role through sensationalized reporting on violent stranger crimes against women and a relative lack of reporting on intimate partner violence. The whole genre of police procedural shows revolves around portrayals of heinous acts of violence against women, each season escalating the imagined crimes and graphic scenes (I'm looking at you, *Criminal Minds* and *Law & Order: svu*). Sexual assault is a common trope throughout movies, books, and television, often used by authors to illustrate a pivotal moment in a woman's character development. Taken together, these portrayals imply that stranger violence and sexual assault are always just around the corner. Comedian Tig Notaro has a bit that captures the effects of this perfectly. Every time a man makes her feel uneasy in public, she wonders, "Is this my rape?" We laugh uneasily because it rings true. We do sort of believe that "our rape" is already out there, an inevitability waiting in the shadows.

In contrast, domestic violence, sexual assault by acquaintances, incest, child abuse, and other "private," yet much more prevalent, crimes receive far less attention. From a feminist perspective, this difference in attention serves to direct women's fear outwards, away from the home and family, reinforcing patriarchal institutions like the nuclear family and women's reliance on heterosexual partnership for the appearance of security. In a vicious cycle, this stigmatizes violence experienced within the "safe" space of the home and drives it further out of sight.

Weighing all of these factors—underreporting, harassment, socialization, media—the paradox of women's fear begins to dissolve. In fact, concludes Whitzman, "women's fear is highly rational."[212] Instead of trying to locate some internal cause or explanation for women's fear, feminists are more interested in situating it within broader structures, systems, and institutions. And this leads to the question, "why is women's fear so deeply embedded, socially and culturally?" The only explanation is that it serves some kind of social function.

It's very Women's Studies 101, but it bears repeating: the social function of women's fear is the control of women. Fear restricts women's lives. It limits our use of public spaces, shapes our choices about work and other economic opportunities, and keeps us, in what is perhaps an *actual* paradox, dependent on men as protectors. This all works to prop up a heteropatriarchal capitalist system in which women are tied to the private space of the home and responsible for domestic labour within the institution of the nuclear family. It's a system that benefits men as a group and upholds the status quo very effectively.

MAPPING DANGER

Where does space come into all of this? What does it have to do with the city? How do social control and geography work together? These questions represent precisely the point where my women's studies background met geography and changed my perspective and my scholarly life forever. Because geography helps us to answer the question *how*. How does gendered social control actually work? How does it play out on the ground and how is it enforced?

Fear of crime surveys ask participants about who they fear, and for women the answer is always men. But men as a group can't practically be avoided. Women's fear of men takes on a geographic logic. We figure out which *places* to avoid, rather than which people. Feminist geographer Gill Valentine explains that this is one way of coping with a constant state of fear: "Women cannot be fearful of all men all the time, therefore in order to maintain an illusion of control over their safety they need to know where and when they may encounter 'dangerous men' in order to avoid them."[213]

Of course, the idea of "dangerous men" isn't purely geographical. Social characteristics come into play, particularly through stereotypes and fear mongering that position groups like men of colour or homeless men as threatening. For women of colour, who report higher levels of harassment and violence than white women, white men and male authority figures such as police officers may be especially worrisome.[214] But since we have very little control over the presence of men in our environments, and can't function in a state of constant fright, we displace some of our fear onto spaces: city streets, alleyways, subway platforms, darkened sidewalks.

These spaces populate our personal mental maps of safety and fear. The map is a living collage, with images, words, and emotions layered over our neighbourhoods and travel routes. The layers come from personal experiences of danger and harassment but also media, rumours, urban myths, and the good old "common sense" that saturates any culture. The map shifts from day to night, weekday to weekend, season to season. Geographer Rachel Pain's research suggests that these geographies of fear change throughout our lives, particularly if we become parents and as we start to age.[215] The map is dynamic. One uncomfortable or scary moment can change it forever.

It's hard to argue with the common-sense notion that it's "natural" for women, as "inherently vulnerable" people, to code the environment in terms of threat and safety. I'm sure someone out there is bound to say it's an evolutionary trait of some kind. But I'm much more interested in questioning the *effects* of being beholden to these maps of danger and what that means for women's lives. And evolution can chew on this for a while: these maps rarely include as dangerous the places where women face the most violence—the home and other private spaces. Instead, threats are externalized onto the urban environment, into parks and laneways and parking garages. Often these spaces are racially coded or classed. Again, it's not that women are irrational or making bad choices. We're accurately reflecting the messages society has drilled into us. The long term and everyday effects, though, are substantial.

Towards the end of my last year of university I got called out to a temporary receptionist job in the east end of Toronto. I was totally unfamiliar with the area, which turned out to be an industrial park, filled with light manufacturing plants and warehouses. There were no sidewalks. I picked my way along the rough roads, trying to avoid glass and nails. My cute office shoes weren't designed for this trek. No one else was walking. I felt incredibly out of place as a young, smartly dressed woman on these streets. After a few days, my boss asked the agency if they could keep me for as long as I was available. Happy to avoid juggling multiple temp jobs for the summer, I agreed. Despite my discomfort, at least the daylight hours were long and I didn't have to walk in the dark. But if this job was offered to me in the fall, or I wanted to keep it long term, I'd have had to factor safety into my choice, and perhaps turn down a solid work opportunity.

THE COST OF FEAR

These are the hidden costs of fear, the ones that keep women from living full, free, and independent lives in the city. The social, psychological, and economic consequences are substantial. They place a tremendous burden on women's already over-loaded days: we have the "double shift" of paid and unpaid work, the triple shift of dealing with racism, homophobia, ableism, etc. on top of sexism, and the quadruple shift of constantly managing our safety.

The endless precautionary measures steal valuable time and energy. Every woman has stories of the time she got off the subway or bus at a distant stop because she worried she was being followed, or took a long and winding route home to ensure she was actually alone. We avoid short cuts through laneways and parks. We vary our travel routes and carry our keys in our fists.

We pretend to be on the phone. We avoid certain places completely. This all adds up to an exhausting set of both routine and spontaneous safety decisions and the need for a constant awareness and attention to safety issues.

The stress generated by a steady, if usually low key, state of uneasiness in the everyday environment is unhealthy and can have long-term ramifications. Recent research suggests that the high levels of stress affect longevity and may even show up as damage to our DNA. It's depressing to decline events or leave early because there's no safe and affordable way home. It's psychologically draining to second guess our choices, wondering if we'll be blamed if something bad happens.[216] Sadly, we're right to worry about this. Studies of media reporting on violence against women—public and domestic—have found that the media implicitly question the survivor's actions, mental health, history, and habits, especially if the victim is Black, Indigenous, or marginalized in some other way.[217]

Economically, these fears have real material outcomes. A better paying night shift or job in a seemingly dangerous area might have to be declined. Night classes that would lead to more training and higher paying jobs might have to be avoided. Affordable housing might be inaccessible if it's in an unsafe area. These costs are rarely accounted for, even when discussing things like the "pink tax." Perhaps more obvious, although still undercounted, are the costs borne when women eschew the cheaper options of cycling or walking in order to avoid harassment. Research shows that in most countries, women walk significantly fewer steps per day than men. It's not laziness. Surveying women in cities like Jakarta, Semarang, Bristol, and Washington, journalist Talia Shadwell found that women often had to run a gauntlet of harassment walking to school or work, prompting them to pay for cabs, ride shares, and buses, even for short distances.[218] Paying for a car, a cell phone, or a building with security are also added financial burdens. For men, these might feel like nice bonuses; for many women, they're necessities. And of course, access to these necessities varies greatly across income, race, ability, and citizenship status.

At the end of the day these limitations and costs and stresses amount to an indirect but highly effective program of social control. Our socially reinforced fears keep us from fully inhabiting the city and from making the most of our lives on a day-to-day basis.

Who benefits from all of this? Doesn't it seem outrageous and even illogical that society would limit women so much? After all, the losses aren't purely born by individuals. One could calculate the lost economic productivity of women due to fear-based choices and see its wider effect on society. But society doesn't function on a purely economic logic, or at least not a logic that supposes or desires an equal playing field for all. The economic logic of a sexist, racist, trans- and homophobic, ableist society operates on the unspoken assumption that economic and other forms of power must first be maximized for white, straight, cis, able-bodied men.

In case that seems a little abstract, think about the repetitive media profiles of the "economic anxiety" plaguing the white working-class man who voted for Trump. The outrage of this group—and the constant moves to appease them or restore some kind of imagined past to satisfy their longings—is premised on the idea that their whiteness and male privilege will always keep them at least one or two socio-economic rungs above women and people of colour. Their belief that this hierarchy is crumbling expresses itself in an often violent backlash against other groups, one that adds yet another layer of fear to the lives of many.

PUSHING BACK

Recognition of both the actual violence women face and the gendered social effects of fear have led feminists to push back in a variety of ways. Movements like Take Back the Night, India's "Pride Strides," Slutwalks, and the #Cuéntelo protests exemplify direct action campaigns insisting on the rights of women and other marginalized groups to urban space. From pushing for simple changes to urban architectural features to advocating for an overhaul of the entire field of urban planning, feminist geographers, planners, anti-violence workers, and others have made substantial, if incomplete, progress toward creating safer, less fearful, cities.

Examples of changes in urban design include alterations to improve lighting, clear obstructed sightlines, and create well-trafficked routes through housing and civic developments. Installation of emergency phone boxes and call buttons in parking garages, parks, and on university campuses can offer an increased sense of safety. In some cities, the widespread use of CCTV has been adopted as a measure meant to reduce crime, although its ability to reduce fear is questionable.[219]

The built environment can be challenging to alter. In old cities like Barcelona, narrow streets, dark corners, stone walls, poor sightlines, and overgrown vegetation create hiding places and a heightened sense of fear. Col-lectiu Punt 6, a feminist cooperative of architects, sociologists, and planners have been trying to increase visibility and remove obstacles in public spaces to increase women's use and enjoyment of space. In Kigali, Rwanda, women working as street vendors have seen their safety, and their economic conditions, improve with the building of secure, permanent mini-markets that include space for breastfeeding.[220]

Around the world, public transit systems are hot beds of harassment and assault for women. In their survey of girls and young women in Lima, Madrid, Kampala, Delhi, and Sydney, NGO Plan International found that public transit was a critical "problem spot" where women reported groping, harassment, and being followed.[221] Although many systems have alarm buttons and "designated waiting areas" on subway platforms, which include call buttons, bright lighting, and CCTV, the crowded and anonymous nature of shared transit remains a problem. Some cities have gone as far as designating women-only train carriages. For example, Tokyo and Osaka have train lines with carriages set aside at particular times for women, disabled people, children, and caregivers. Mexico City, Cairo, and Tehran have similar accommodations. Of course, critics point out that simply segregating women doesn't require men to change their behaviour or attitudes.

Technology is also being used in the form of apps that make reporting harassment on public transit simpler. For example, Vancouver's "Project Global Guardian" app allows passengers to text police and public transit officers directly. In Melbourne, a safety app is being developed in consultation with girls and women who use public transit. Cities such as Stockholm and Geneva have banned sexist advertising and objectifying images of women in their transit systems, recognizing the harm of negative stereotypes and their role in creating harassment-prone environments.

These changes didn't come about naturally. Women were pushing for cities to take gendered concerns, especially safety, seriously. But getting municipalities and specifically urban planners to listen to the experiences of women and other vulnerable citizens has been an uphill battle. Planning considers itself an objective, rational, and scientific field of study and practice. It's oriented toward managing or encouraging growth and development and to providing services to a faceless imagined "citizen." The idea that social differences such as gender, race, and sexuality could and should be taken into account was literally laughed at when feminist planners and groups like Women Plan Toronto brought gendered issues to the planning table in the 1980s and 1990s.[222] Often, it takes a high profile public act of violence against women to spur cities into action.

In Delhi, the horrific sexual assault and murder of student Jyoti Singh on a bus in 2012 made international headlines and brought women out into the streets in protest, demanding attention to their safety. Women's organizations succeeded in getting some space in Toronto's municipal sphere only after several violent public assaults against women caught the city's attention in the 1980s, although city councillor Kristyn Wong-Tam notes that the safer city guidelines have not been updated since the late 1990s.[223] In most cases, women's organizations still have to take matters into their own hands to create change. In Delhi, Kalpana Viswanath created the SafetiPin app, which collects safety-related data from women and also allows them to have a trusted friend track their journeys. The app has spread to many other cities and is being used in coordination with city authorities in places like Hanoi and Bogotá.[224]

SafetiPin is like a high-tech version of the safety audit, a tool created by Toronto's Metro Toronto Action Committee on Violence Against Women and Children (METRAC) in an effort to figure out new ways to get planners and bureaucrats to listen to women's experiences. Critically, the safety audit insists that it's the people who live, work, study, and play in these spaces who are the experts on safety and danger. Community members go on "walkabouts," collecting information on factors like lighting and sightlines. They also record experiential elements including how, where, and why feelings of danger may arise. Safety audits are used in cities around the world now, with the goal of empowering community members to generate specific recommendations for changes.[225]

How far can these changes to the built environment and new technological interventions take us? The "crime prevention through environmental design," or CPTED, school of thought suggests that since much crime is opportunistic in nature, reducing opportunities is critical. Oscar Newman's CPTED approach is well known for his concept of "defensible space," the idea that physical characteristics such as building architecture and site layout will allow residents to be active in crime prevention by giving them a sense of control and territoriality.[226] These kinds of approaches assume a tight link between the physical environment and human behaviour and a certain predictability in criminal behaviour that can be mitigated by design changes. If design was the answer though, surely, we'd have designed out crime by now?

Unfortunately, CPTED relies on a rather mechanistic understanding of space and fear, assuming that fear will follow a rational trajectory and decrease when safety improvements are made. Fear, however, is much more complex and people's emotions in general don't respond in easily predictable ways. Perhaps most importantly, feminist critics of this approach have highlighted the fact that "it is impossible to speak of reactions to the threat of crime in particular environments without taking into account the social and political relations which structure both the physical environment, and the daily lives, of the individuals involved."[227] In other words, we can't detach the social world from the built environment.

This complexity seems to stymy urban designers. Feminist qualitative work on women's fear in cities reveals what seem like contradictory and insurmountable claims: women are afraid in enclosed and open spaces; in busy places and empty places; on transit and while walking; isolated under a bright light or invisible in the dark.[228] What's a criminologist or urban planner to do?

Whitzman recalls the brush-offs she received from city planners when presenting her research on women's fear in urban green spaces: "What do you want to do? Pave parks?"[229] And feminist geographers Hille Koskela and Rachel Pain's research revealed that planners were at a loss once their attempts to widen walkways and improve lighting failed to significantly increase feelings of safety: "What is there left to try?"[230]

When I teach this material, this is usually the point at which my geography students get really discouraged or really annoyed. They were so hopeful thinking about environmental and design solutions. And then they realize that no amount of lighting is going abolish the patriarchy. "So, what are the answers?" they sulk, frustrated that the authors we read are often just as discouraged by their research findings. It's true: there are no straightforward solutions. Any attempt to improve urban safety has to grapple with social, cultural, and economic elements as well as the form of the built environment.

The failure to imagine different kinds of interventions speaks to the disconnect between what typical fear of crime surveys reveal and women's everyday realities. Surveys tend to deal with a simplified and narrow concept of "fear of crime," and they either implicitly or explicitly assume crime that occurs in public spaces. As we know, though, women's fear of crime is informed by a much broader and deeper set of fears and experiences, from street harassment, childhood abuse, domestic abuse, socialization, media, and the specific nature of sexual crimes which are imbued with their own special horror. Fear is also contoured by differences across age, race, class, sexuality, gender identity, and ability. So, while feminists have certainly campaigned for changes to the built environment, they've never lost sight of the fact that women's lack of safety exists within an interlocking network of domination that facilitates the social control of women and other less powerful groups in the city. Under these conditions, fear can never simply be "designed out."

BOLD WOMEN

It's hard to overestimate the effect of daily fear. Even when fear isn't actively present, the burden of a set of routinized precautions is always there, although they're so naturalized that we barely notice we're doing them. What's amazing, and typically overlooked, is the fact that women constantly defy their fears and act in ways that are brave, empowered, and liberating in cities.

Women still jog through Central Park. Women ride the bus at night. Women walk home alone at 3 a.m. when the bar closes. Women open their windows on hot summer nights. Yet women's fear is believed to be so deeply ingrained (even if some call it irrational) that discussions of courage, wisdom, and good sense are rare and easily discounted as false outward displays of bravado. Moreover, women find it incredibly difficult to acknowledge their own bravery and clear judgment.

Hille Koskela writes about what she calls "female boldness and defiance," asking "what can be gained by analyzing women's courage and their ability to take possession of space?"[231] Koskela's research with women in Helsinki demonstrated that women can act boldly and even without fear, however, even unafraid women frequently have a voice in the back of their heads that says, "maybe you should be afraid here," even when there are no signs of danger or threat.

Koskela notes another fascinating phenomenon: even when women's decisions to act bravely work out well (i.e., no harm comes to them), they don't interpret these moments as signs that they've made well-informed, rational choices based on experience, the data at hand, and their own gut instincts. Rather, they re-interpret the situation as one where they did something "stupid," but "got away with it."

Wow, did her observation ever hit home for me. I was blown away by its simple accuracy and its implications for how society views women's choices and how we understand our own capabilities, intellects, and instincts. Every story I tell of an urban adventure—staying out all night in the city with my friend, hitchhiking home during the great 2003 blackout—ends with something like, "That was so stupid! I'm lucky I'm not dead in a ditch!" When I was interviewing women for my master's thesis, they told me story after story of "taking possession" of urban space, only to dismiss their abilities as "luck," shaking their heads in disbelief at the risks they'd taken.

What if we reframed these experiences as moments when we correctly processed all the available information and made a wise, calculated choice? Women know how to use the instincts we've honed living in a hostile, patriarchal climate, as well as ultra-sensitive emotional and rational processing abilities. Having to navigate a male-dominated world cultivates these skills. Thinking this way completely shifts things. For the most part, women aren't walking around being lucky. We're walking around being smart, bold, experienced, and wise. If we reject or dismiss women's claims of bravery, we quickly run the risk of denying women's agency and ability to know themselves. That's hardly a feminist take on the matter.

This isn't to say that anyone who experiences violence or harm has "made bad choices." Not at all. Only perpetrators are responsible for the harm they cause. And women are socialized to ignore our guts and hearts and minds on so many occasions. We're taught to be nice, to not cause conflict. And we often believe that acting nice will protect us from threats because we've seen how abuse escalates when women say no, ignore men, or walk away from an uncomfortable situation. It's an internal wrestling match between our own instincts and knowledge, social conditioning, fear of being too fearful (e.g. "paranoid"), and our all-too-common memories of past violence. With so many conflicting messages, it's difficult to trust ourselves, even when we've made good decisions.

I'm also not suggesting that the solution to fear of crime is for women to get better at following our guts. This would do little to reduce the greatest threat women face: violence from known men in the home, school, and workplace. And, indeed, this remains a major stumbling block for anyone thinking about improving safety for women. Public and design interventions rarely address private violence. The perceived separation between public and private also means that these problems tend to be addressed independently, without much thought to how public and private (themselves vastly oversimplified social and spatial categories) influence and produce one another.[232] Feminist geographers have made some important interventions here but the scale and complexity of violence against women is challenging. However, scale and complexity aren't excuses for throwing our hands up in the face of a problem. What is clear is that whatever interventions we produce have to take into account the spatial and the social, public and private, and above all, they must be intersectional.

INTERSECTIONALITY AND VIOLENCE

While gender-based violence may be a common denominator, other markers of social location always shape the particular kinds of violence, harassment, and danger that women encounter. And these aren't separable. A woman who has her hijab ripped off cannot be asked to choose whether it was sexist or Islamophobic violence. The massive scale and historical longevity of violence against Indigenous women isn't reducible to just one of racism, colonialism, or sexism. As Indigenous women have long argued, gendered violence is a key tool of settler colonialism, one that continues to be wielded by both the state and individuals within the nation.[233]

The horrors of child migrant detention succeeded in capturing our attention at the end of 2018 and into 2019, showing how the state terrorizes those without formal immigration status in order to deter people, especially women, from seeking asylum. Women with disabilities face some of the highest levels of physical and sexual abuse everywhere. And trans women of colour, especially those who may be involved in sex work, are killed at an astonishing rate. In all of these examples, gender and gender identity are salient but gendered violence interlocks with other forms of violence in every situation.

In the city, public violence and fear of crime are often addressed as single-issue problems, e.g. as "women's problems." This creates limited forms of intervention, some of which are doomed to fail because they lack consideration of women's multiple social locations. Efforts to increase policing, add lighting, and install CCTV are likely to make the streets more dangerous for sex workers, who not only risk arrest and violence from the police, but who are pushed into less safe locations to work. Women without formal immigration status or who don't speak the local language well may not feel comfortable accessing services or spaces designed to make women safer.[234] Even asking to be let off the bus in between stops could be a huge hurdle. And the widespread lack of physically accessible spaces for disabled people means that disabled women are highly constrained in the kinds of choices they can make about safety. Thus, any policies, practices, and design changes meant to increase safety must take a hard look at how different members of society will be affected. It may be impossible to find a one-size-fits-all solution, but we still have to take an intersectional approach whenever possible.

It's also true that relying on cities to have women's backs hasn't worked out all that well. I'm thinking of the disturbingly widespread practice of altering police statistics to make crimes against women, especially sexual assaults, disappear. In the 1990s, the Philadelphia police force was found to have been manipulating crime data in order to make the city—especially the rapidly gentrifying central city—seem safer than it actually was. Geographer Alec Brownlow's research into this case showed that for decades, the police deliberately misrepresented reports of sexual violence, especially rape, by categorizing these reports as either "unfounded" or simply "investigation of person."[235] Up to one third of crimes had been miscoded. Connecting gentrification and gender violence, Winifred Curran notes that by making rape invisible, Philadelphia could market itself as one of the best and safest cities for young, single professionals, including women.[236]

In 2017, Canadian reporter Robyn Doolittle exposed the shockingly common use of the "unfounded" label by police forces across the country, sparking reviews of this practice in almost every jurisdiction. Some 37,000 cases were reopened (Doolittle 2017b).[237] Doolittle's work revealed the prevalence of rape myths among detectives who seemed to have little understanding of trauma, victim blaming, and the dynamics of acquaintance rape. It further illustrated that while lack of reporting keeps violence against women hidden, reporting violence may do little to help change the situation. The true extent of gender-based violence remains unknown in part because our institutions seem highly invested in minimizing these crimes.

The stories uncovered by Brownlow and Doolittle make my blood pressure skyrocket whenever I think of them. I had to stop typing and do a load of laundry just to calm down enough to share their findings. The "unfounded" investigations are a painful reminder that cities are rarely dedicated to becoming truly safer for women. Instead, the appearance of safety comes to stand in for the end goal.

Making cities *seem* safe for women also tends to make them less safe for other marginalized groups. Efforts to "clean up" downtown areas and "revitalize" residential and retail districts are typically accomplished through a combination of aesthetic measures (beautification projects) and the active removal of groups of people that have been marked as symbols of disorder, danger, crime, or disease. Historically, entire communities of people of colour, especially Black people, were razed in the name of urban renewal, including Halifax's Africville and Vancouver's Hogan's Alley. Today, less overt practices involve the targeting of homeless people and sex workers through criminalization. Youth, particularly youth of colour, are heavily policed via carding practices and over-arrested. Spaces that serve disadvantaged communities and recent immigrants are closed, moved, or under-resourced in order push the poor, working class, and racialized out of these "regenerating areas."

The readiness of white folks, including white women, to call the cops on people of colour makes them effective agents of this policing. What has come to be called "carceral feminism" is partly to blame: a version of anti-violence work that calls for harsh punishments and relies on the police and criminal justice system to solve gender-based violence.[238] In her book *Arrested Justice: Black Women, Violence, and America's Prison Nation*,[239] African American Studies professor Beth Richie notes that while some women have seen their safety improve over the last few decades, women with less power are "in as much danger as ever, precisely because of the ideological and strategic direction the anti-violence movement has taken during the buildup of America's prison nation." In a context where the criminal justice system is deeply racist and classist, a carceral approach can only serve to deepen inequalities and continually re-stigmatize and overly target the households of Black and Indigenous people and people of colour. Carceral feminism unwittingly participates in a system where police and cities are actually doing very little to improve women's safety, but can use women's safety as a justification for policies and practices that target other vulnerable groups and make them more susceptible to state and street violence.

In my research on gender and condominium development in Toronto, I found that developers and real estate agents enthusiastically marketed condos to women with the idea that the 24-hour concierge and security staff, as well as technical features such as handprint locks, CCTV, and alarm systems, made condos the safest option for women living downtown.[240] These features were highly touted when condos were arriving in "up and coming" neighbourhoods that had previously been stigmatized or seen as abandoned, industrial areas. I argued then that by making condos "safe" for women, developers were smoothing their path to expansion into neighbourhoods that might otherwise have been risky real estate investments. This expansion certainly wasn't going to make life any safer for the women who would be displaced by this form of gentrification. Nor does it tackle domestic violence in any way. Furthermore, asking women to "buy" their safety through condo ownership contributes to the trend of privatization, where people are held responsible for their own well-being, even their safety from crime. Making safety a private commodity in the city means that it becomes less and less available to those who lack the economic means to secure themselves. This is certainly a long way from an intersectional feminist vision of a safer city for women.

We may not know exactly what a safe city looks like, but we know that it won't involve private safety measures. It won't rely on the police to prevent or adequately investigate crimes. It won't throw sex workers, people of colour, youth, or immigrants under the bus to create the appearance of safety. It won't be centred on the needs and desires of privileged white women. And it won't expect physical changes to undo patriarchal dominance.

At a minimum, an intersectional approach that starts from the needs and perspectives of the most vulnerable will be required. Listening to and believing women will be standard practice. An understanding of the interconnections between private and public violence will increase. Rape myths and rape culture will be dismantled. Fear will not be a tactic of social control. In a safe, feminist city, women won't have to be courageous just to step outside the door. Our energies won't be wasted on a million and one safety precautions. In this city, the full extent of what women have to offer the world can be realized.

CITY OF POSSIBILITY

My earliest memories of cities like Toronto, London, and New York are impressionistic, often nostalgic, with fleeting recollections of sounds, smells, atmospheres, and bodily sensations. As I grew older, these feelings drew me to university in the biggest city in Canada, to moving to London, and to making a living studying cities. When I arrive back in the city today, something in my body shifts and a kind of urban muscle memory takes over. I step off a train and emerge onto a busy city street and my posture changes, my gait alters, my facial expression is different. Ten years of small town life mean that I probably make a little more eye contact with strangers than I once would have, but my body still knows how to move through the city.

I started writing about the feminist city through the questions generated by women's embodied experiences of city life. The "geography closest in" is solid material from which to question all that we take for granted in cities. And because so many of the ways that women are cast as problems for cities revolve around our bodies—too fat, too fertile, too sexual, too messy, too vulnerable—we must keep returning to the body to help us imagine alternatives. Feminist urban activists and scholars pay attention to the body with a careful understanding that the body is a site where gendered, classed, raced, and sexualized urban power relations and politics play out.[241] While my own embodied experiences aren't universal, I know they resonate because women have been talking and writing and sometimes shouting about these issues ever since urban life became a pressing social concern.

The city for women can be a real minefield, but as Rebecca Traister writes, it can also be a "true love," furnishing women with all the support that traditional marriage was meant to provide and a great deal more freedom to boot.[242] Looking at my daughter now, I delight in her confidence and joy in the city. She moved to Montréal at eighteen, a city she barely knew. On the phone, she's gleeful about her new metro pass: "I love being able to go anywhere!" When I visit, she walks with the speed and intensity of a born-and-bred urbanite, too fast even for me. I want her to be brave and brash, I want her to take up space here. I don't let my mind wander too often through the dreadful scenarios every parent occasionally conjures. And I certainly don't burden her with my fears, although we've had many candid talks about safety, bystander interventions, and rape culture, topics she understands far better than I did at eighteen. I do wonder what she doesn't tell me about. My own experiences suggest that I already know the answers to those unspoken questions. But I don't want any of that to stop her from loving her urban life.

Nonetheless, she's learning that being a woman alone in the city means learning a set of embodied habits, mostly unconsciously. Over time and through repetition (or iteration, as Judith Butler would say[243]) these condense and shape the body. Your posture, walk, facial expressions, movements, gestures, eye contact, stance, muscle tension, and more are moulded by navigating the urban environment—the city of men—and the social relations that swirl within it. Your body "keeps the score" of moments of fear, harassment, violence, and unwanted contact.[244] It holds onto that sense of shock, the recoil, the disgust, and the anger that accompany deliberate, uninvited touch. Moments when fight or flight impulses kick in make stark imprints. The visceral discomfort of sexualizing, objectifying comments and the accompanying shame and impotent rage are held just below the surface of the skin. Sometimes they're so close to the surface that reactions like cursing and rude gestures turn into reflexes. When I moved to a small town, I had to fight this reflex when I heard a honk or a holler to avoid giving dear unsuspecting colleagues and neighbours the finger. But decades of city life had taught my body not to trust public space.

I hate that I've been socialized to react this way. Not because I envision a city where strangers are freely in extensive amounts of physical and other forms of contact with one another. But this distrust bleeds into other aspects of city life and less "touchy" forms of urban contact. The urge to keep a safe bubble around myself, to exert as much control as possible over my personal space, might mean that I'm less open to other kinds of experiences, relationships, and encounters. This sense of enclosure gets shaped by classed, racialized, and sexualized ideas about cleanliness, disease, contagion, and questions about who is worthy of interaction. Will I reach out to offer money or food to someone experiencing homelessness? Offer assistance to someone who appears unwell or hurt? Volunteer with sex workers or an HIV/AIDS organization? Ally with trans people? Send my kid to school in a racially diverse neighbourhood? Attend yoga classes for people of all body sizes and abilities? Participate in a pow wow or a round dance?

I'm not suggesting that gendered fear directly leads to fear of all kinds of encounters across difference, or that it justifies any kind of bigotry. But it doesn't help break down barriers. When you've experienced fear or trauma, when strangers have tried to make demands on your personal space and physical body, you hold something back. You don't feel as free to seek out different kinds of contact, to open yourself to experiencing new environments, or to offer a piece of yourself to the world. You might find yourself secretly or not so secretly desiring that SUV to protect yourself against contact.[245] It might seem natural to want to live in a condo with 24-hour security. It might feel more comfortable to choose a neighbourhood where people look, talk, and act like you. Women of course need to challenge these impulses. We need to recognize that the social control of women through socialization into fear is part of a system that seeks to enforce other forms of exclusion, segregation, and fear of difference. But breaking down these systems will be all the more difficult in a city where women experience harassment, objectification, limitations, and real violence.

While I harbour no illusions that urban public spaces of the past were consistently delightful for women, queer folks, Black and Indigenous people, or people of colour, recent decades have brought palpable but not positive changes to the possibilities for spontaneous, non-threatening encounters across difference. The science fiction writer Samuel R. Delany writes about the transformation of Times Square in the 1980s and 1990s from a place of queer contact, "licentious and loud," to a Disney-fied consumption space, made clean and safe for the middle classes and tourists.[246] Eschewing nostalgia, Delany nonetheless seeks to chronicle his memories of street life, local hustlers, porn theatres, and the overall vibe of an area that was probably the first to experience a full metamorphosis under Mayor Rudy Giuliani's zero tolerance "clean up" campaign in the 1990s. Delany recalls not only the spaces for gay male sexual contact along Forty-Second Street, but also the racially diverse community, vibrant street life, and inexpensive sites for food, drinks, and entertainment.

Feminist geographer and filmmaker Brett Story aptly describes Delany's memoir as "a treatise about contact with strangers at the margins of 'family values' and spectacle tourism."[247] In her own writing, Story makes the case that "contact at the margins" in cities is a form of transgression against forces of capitalism that police contact across difference. This contact might be transformative of social relations in the city. But in the "city of capital ... the city that belongs to no one"[248] where bland and neutral spaces, a sense of constant danger, and over-surveillance and over-policing hold sway, ordinary sorts of contact are increasingly unlikely and fraught with anxiety.

In this context, embodied markers of difference serve as bat-signals for cities to encourage redevelopment, gentrification, and hyper-policing. In changing neighbourhoods, the ways bodies inhabit and move through space tell us a lot about who belongs. Subtle habits of stance, making (or not making) eye contact, gait, tone of voice, the way one eats, and so much more signify the cultural and social markers of belonging and exclusion.[249] For example, the body of the yoga mum or the bearded hipster has come to signify gentrification.[250] Bodies that do not conform due to age, illness, disability, racialization, class, sexuality, addiction, etc., are marked as "out of place" and targeted for displacement.

This dynamic is incredibly common in gentrifying areas and facilitated by new technologies. Private social network apps like "Nextdoor" allow neighbours to report on those who seem suspicious and to target people and businesses for everything from the smell of the cooking to the kind of music they play. Not surprisingly, it's white gentrifiers who are reporting their neighbours of colour and long-term residents and businesses through these new technologies. Investigating the fatal shooting of Alex Nieto in the gentrifying Bernal Heights district of San Francisco after white men walking their dogs reported him as suspicious (he was eating a burrito on a park bench before work), Rebecca Solnit writes that people of colour become seen as "menaces and intruders in their own neighbourhood," facing evictions, police violence, and perhaps even death.[251]

The embodied politics of displacement, danger, and death remind me that there's a lot to be concerned about when trying to bring a feminist perspective to questions of contact, transformation, and different urban futures. It's tempting to say that none of this is possible without first ensuring the safety of women in cities. However, the means to that end favoured in the era of neoliberal urbanism, such as heightened state and corporate surveillance, militarized policing, and the privatization of public space, are just as likely to decrease safety for others. These measures likewise do little or nothing to address the greatest threat to women's safety, namely violence in private spaces.

It's also tempting to lean on measures of economic equality as solutions. Certainly, affordable housing, living wages, free child care, and affordable health care and education are critical ingredients for most feminist urban visions. But far too much Marxist and "critical" scholarship and activism places gender, race, sexuality, and disability at the margins of the struggle, with the faulty assumption that once the economic side is settled, everything else will sort itself out.[252] But failures to really think about care work and social reproduction, not to mention gender-based violence, mean that relying too heavily on economic solutions isn't likely to be as transformative as we might hope.

These economic visions rarely grapple with settler colonialism or the possibilities for decolonization in the city. In settler colonial states like Canada, the U.S., or Australia, it's well past time for all urban planning decisions about space to involve Indigenous nations. While large-scale decolonization might be a long way off, urban land transfers and urban reserves are methods through which Indigenous control of colonized city spaces can be regained.[253] At the more everyday level, addressing the violence faced by Indigenous women in cities through a deep understanding of the nexus of misogyny and structural settler violence is crucial to advancing any attempt at urban reconciliation.

Looking to the past is also a limited option. Although some urbanists seem nostalgic for a time before smartphones, when street life was more sociable and the chance encounters described by Delany were more likely, the reality is that this Jane Jacobs-esque scene hid a wide range of exclusions across race, class, ability, and sexuality. James Baldwin wrote about the same neighbourhoods as Jacobs, where as a queer Black man he was regularly harassed by the police and viewed as a dangerous outsider, rather than part of the delightful diversity of Jacobs' own version of Greenwich Village.[254] While I think we can learn some valuable lessons from looking at neighbourhoods prior to gentrification or urban renewal, we need to set aside the rose-coloured glasses and notice who is missing from that picture of idealized city life.

Where do we begin? For one, the faces of urban planning, politics, and architecture have to change. A wider range of lived experience needs to be represented among those who make the decisions that have enormous effects on people's everyday lives. An intersectional analysis must be a common approach to decisions big and small: where to place a new elementary school, how far apart bus stops will be, whether small businesses can be operated out of homes, etc. In global south cities, foreign NGOs and local authorities need to amplify the voices of women who best know what changes will improve their lives. Indigenous peoples' interests need to be represented. Planning to improve safety for women can't reproduce carceral models that target poor people and people of colour.

I want to insist that feminist visions of the city have been here all along. Some were never fully realized and some are in the past, but there are examples of both practices and ideals that are being lived right now, under our noses. What might exist as pockets of resistance or simply alternative ways of organizing care, work, food, and more are sites of possibility for a broader, transformative vision. Sites such as Copenhagen's *Send Flere Krydderier* (Send More Spices) café at the *Verdenskulturcentret* (Centre for Cultures of the World), where immigrant women prepare food for sale, share their stories through art, and connect to the community. My friend and colleague Heather McLean writes about Glasgow's Kinning Park Complex, a community organization in a working class, racialized neighbourhood where solidarity amongst recent immigrants and working class neighbours results in community meals, repair cafés, and vibrant performances.[255] In my old Toronto neighbourhood, the Junction, scholar-artist-activists Kim Jackson and Nancy Viva Davis Halifax facilitate the Monday Night Art Group in the Evangeline Women's Shelter. Visiting with the group for a few weeks one summer, I experienced how Kim, Nancy, and all of the women who participate create something different out of, in the collective's words, "the neoliberal conditions of poverty" that shape the shelter experience:

> MAG is a space where women work on their own projects, develop skills, make gifts or practical items, share and produce knowledge and spend time with one another, in other words MAG is an informal economic space of affective, knowledge, informational, supportive, resource, and gifting exchanges. The MAG is also a performative space where we push the boundaries of neighbourliness, of social arts, dialogue and resistance.[256]

On a wider stage, women are leading some of the most transformative social movements of our time, ones that are shifting the kinds of conversations we can have about the future of cities and urban life. Black Lives Matter challenges everything we think we believe about policing, safety, crime, and danger and their connections to deeply gendered issues such as social housing, gentrification, local government, and more. Idle No More, an environmental movement led by Indigenous women, successfully brought Indigenous and non-Indigenous allies together in protests and round dance events in cities across Canada, opening up new channels for wider understandings of how environmental issues must be a site of widespread solidarity.

The Fight for $15 campaign, a women-led movement to establish livable wages for underpaid workers in cities around the world, started with workers walking off their jobs in New York City in 2012. Describing themselves as "fast-food workers, home health aides, child care teachers, airport workers, adjunct professors, retail employees—and underpaid workers everywhere," this movement supports a highly-feminized and racialized work-force whose low wages, long hours, and precarious working conditions (including rampant sexual harassment) deeply affect the lives of women and their families everywhere.[257] In the U.K., the women of the Focus E15 Campaign, or the "E15 Mums" as they were known, refused to vacate their social housing when their local London council decided to tear it down. They were told they'd have to disperse to social housing in other cities. Protesting a "city-wide process of social cleansing, with low income people being forced to the fringes of London and beyond by soaring rents, benefit cuts, and a shortage of social housing," their campaign has spread widely since 2013.[258] In a context where the majority of social housing tenants are women, in the U.K. and elsewhere, this group has worked to raise awareness of how the massive redevelopment of social housing into gentri-fied market housing affects women.

These movements and many, many others are already enacting visions of the feminist city. These visions ask us to think about new ways to organize paid work, care work, and social reproduction. Importantly, they don't rely on the heterosexual nuclear family as the default basis for organizing these relations. They don't rely on the family or men as sources of economic and physical protection for women, although they recognize the importance of allowing people to create and nurture their own kinship structures. They recognize women's autonomy but also our connectedness, to our friends, our communities, our movements. They invite solidarity from everyone who wants to feel safe in their homes, on the streets, in the bathroom, at work, and at school. They recognize the inter-sections of gendered concerns with multiple other systems of privilege and oppression, refusing a feminism where raising the status of privileged white women is the marker of success.

The feminist city doesn't need a blueprint to make it real. I don't want a feminist super-planner to tear everything down and start again. But once we begin to see how the city is set up to sustain a particular way of organizing society—across gender, race, sexuality, and more—we can start to look for new possibilities. There are different ways of using the urban spaces we have. There are endless options for creating alternative spaces. There are little feminist cities sprouting up in neighbourhoods all over the place, if we can only learn to recognize and nurture them. The feminist city is an aspirational project, one without a "master" plan that in fact resists the lure of mastery. The feminist city is an ongoing experiment in living differently, living better, and living more justly in an urban world.

NOTES

PREFACE

1   Helen Lewis, "The Coronavirus is a Disaster for Feminism," *The Atlantic*, March 19, 2020, https://www.theatlantic.com/international/archive/2020/03/feminism-womens-rights-coronavirus-covid19/.

2   Koa Beck, "Don't Call the Pandemic a Setback for Feminism," *Time*, December 23, 2020, https://time.com/5923763/white-feminism-pandemic/.

3   Alisha Haridasani Gupta, "Why Some Women Call This Recession a 'Shecession'," *New York Times*, May 9, 2020, https://www.nytimes.com/2020/05/09/us/unemployment-coronavirus-women.html.

4   William Wan, Tara Bahrampour and Julianne McShane, "U.S. Birthrate Falls to its Lowest Level in Decades in Wake of Pandemic," *The Washington Post*, May 5, 2021, https://www.washingtonpost.com/health/2021/05/05/birth-rate-falls-pandemic/.

5   Hawaii State Commission on the Status of Women, *Building Bridges, Not Walking on Backs: A Feminist Economic Recovery Plan for COVID-19*. April 14, 2020, p. 1.

6   Mariame Kaba, *We Do This 'Til We Free Us: Abolitionist Organizing and Transforming Justice* (Chicago: Haymarket Books, 2021); Lola Olufemi, *Feminism Interrupted: Disrupting Power* (London: Pluto Press, 2020).

7   World Health Organization, *Violence Against Women*, March 9, 2021, https://www.who.int/news-room/fact-sheets/detail/violence-against-women/.

1   Elizabeth Wilson, *The Sphinx in the City: Urban Life, the Control of Disorder, and Women* (Berkeley: University of California Press, 1991), 29.

2   Judith R. Walkowitz, *City of Dreadful Delight: Narratives of Sexual Danger in Late-Victorian London* (Chicago: The University of Chicago Press, 1992), 11.

3   Wilson, 27.

4   Wilson, 39.

5   Lee Maracle, *I Am Woman: A Native Perspective on Sociology and Feminism* (Vancouver: Press Gang, 1996); Andrea Smith, *Conquest: Sexual Violence and American Indian Genocide* (Cambridge: South End Press, 2005).

6   Sarah Hunt, "Representing Colonial Violence: Trafficking, Sex Work, and the Violence of Law," *Atlantis*, 37.2,1 (2015/2016): 25–39.

7   University of Toronto Magazine, *The Cities We Need*, Autumn 2018.

8   Sara Ahmed, "White Men," *feministkilljoys*, accessed January 28, 2019, https://feministkilljoys.com/2014/11/04/white-men/ (original emphasis).

9   Adrienne Rich, *Blood, Bread, and Poetry: Selected Prose 1979–1985* (New York: W.W. Norton, 1994).

10   Rich, 213.

11   Rich, 216.

12   A group originally created by activist Tarana Burke in 2005; "#MeToo" exploded as a Twitter hashtag in 2017.

13   For example, over 150 women testified to abuse at the hands of Larry Nasser, a doctor for elite U.S. gymnasts and college athletes.

14   Gerda Wekerle, "A Woman's Place is in the City," *Antipode*, 16,3 (1984): 11–19.

15   Elizabeth Stanko, "Women, Crime, and Fear," *Annals of the American Academy of Political and Social Science*, 539,1 (1995): 46–58.

16   Wilson, *The Sphinx in the City*, 31.

17   Charlotte Brontë, *Villette* (1853), cited in Wilson, *The Sphinx in the City*, 30.

18   Leslie Kern, "Selling the 'Scary City': Gendering Freedom, Fear and Condominium Development in the Neoliberal City," *Social & Cultural Geography*, 11,3 (2010): 209–230.

19   Margaret Wente wrote a weekly column in Canada's national *Globe & Mail* newspaper from 1986 to 2019.

20   Jane Darke, "The Man-Shaped City," in *Changing Places: Women's Lives in the City*, eds. Chris Booth, Jane Darke and Sue Yeandle (London: Sage, 1996), 88 (my emphasis).

21   Caroline Criado Perez, *Invisible Women: Data Bias in a World Designed for Men* (New York: Abrams, 2019).

22   Oliver Moore, "The 'Baked-In Biases' of the Public Square: Calls Grow to Redesign Cities with Women in Mind," *The Globe and Mail*, April 1, 2019, https://www.theglobeandmail.com/canada/toronto/article-designing-safer-cities-for-women/.

23 Dolores Hayden, "Skyscraper Seduction, Skyscraper Rape," *Heresies*, 2 (May 1977): 108–115.

24 Liz Bondi, "Gender Symbols and Urban Landscapes," *Progress in Human Geography*, 16,2 (1992): 160.

25 Bondi, 160.

26 Janice Monk and Susan Hanson, "On Not Excluding Half of the Human in Human Geography," *The Professional Geographer*, 34 (1982): 11–23.

27 Kimberlé Crenshaw, "Demarginalizing the Intersection of Race and Sex: A Black Feminist Critique of Antidiscrimination Doctrine, Feminist Theory, and Antiracist Politics," in *Feminist Legal Theory: Readings In Law And Gender*, eds. Katherine Bartlett and Roseanne Kennedy (New York: Routledge, 1991); Patricia Hill Collins, *Black Feminist Thought: Knowledge, Consciousness, and the Politics of Empowerment*, 2nd Edition (New York: Routledge, 2000); bell hooks, *Feminist Theory: From Margin to Center*, 2nd Edition (Cambridge: South End Press, 2000).

28 Gill Valentine, "'Sticks and Stones May Break My Bones': A Personal Geography of Harassment," *Antipode*, 30,4 (1998): 305–332; Laura Pulido, "Reflections on a White Discipline," *The Professional Geographer*, 54,1 (2002): 42–49; Audrey Kobayashi, "Coloring the Field: Gender, 'Race,' and the Politics of Fieldwork," *The Professional Geographer*, 46,1 (1994): 73–80; Katherine McKittrick, *Demonic Grounds: Black Women and the Cartographies of Struggle* (Minneapolis: University of Minnesota Press, 2006).

29 Donna Haraway, "Situated Knowledges: The Science Question in Feminism and the Privilege of Partial Perspective," *Feminist Studies* 14,3 (1988): 575–599.

30 Linda Peake and Martina Rieker, eds., *Rethinking Feminist Interventions into the Urban* (London: Routledge, 2013).

31 Charles Baudelaire, *The Painter of Modern Life*, (New York: Da Capo Press, 1964). Orig. published in *Le Figaro*, in 1863.

32 Walter Benjamin, *The Arcades Project*, ed. Rolf Tiedemann, trans. Howard Eiland and Kevin McLaughlin (Cambridge: Belknap Press, 1999); Georg Simmel, "The Metropolis and Mental Life," adapt. D. Weinstein from trans. Kurt Wolff in *The Sociology of Georg Simmel* (New York: Free Press, 1950): 409–424.

33 Janet Wolff, "The Invisible Flâneuse: Women and the Literature of Modernity," *Theory, Culture, and Society*, 3 (1985): 37–46.

34 Virginia Woolf, "Street Haunting: A London Adventure," in *Volume IV Collected Essays* (New York: Harcourt, Brace and World, Inc., 1930): 166.

35 Virginia Woolf, *The Diary of Virginia Woolf* (London: Hogarth Press, 1977).

36 Sally Munt, "The Lesbian Flâneur," in *The Unknown City: Contesting Architecture and Social Space*, eds. Iain Borden, Joe Kerr, Jane Rendell with Alicia Pavaro (Cambridge: MIT Press, 2000): 247–262

37 Lauren Elkin, *Flâneuse: Women Walk the City in Paris, New York, Tokyo, Venice, and London* (New York: Farrar, Strauss and Giroux, 2016), chap 1: Flâneuseing, Kindle.

38 Elkin, *Flâneuse.*

39 Katerie Gladdys, "Stroller Flâneur," *Wagadu*, 7 (Today's Global Flâneuse, 2011), 84–85.

40 Anna Quindlen, "The Ignominy of Being Pregnant in New York City," *New York Times*, March 27, 1996, https://www.nytimes.com/1986/03/27/garden/hers-the-ignominy-of-being-pregnant-in-new-york-city.html.

41 Wekerle, "A Woman's Place is in the City."

42 Betty Friedan, *The Feminine Mystique* (New York: W.W. Norton & Company, Inc., 1997 (1963): 57.

43 Dolores Hayden, *Redesigning the American Dream: Gender, Housing, and Family Life* (New York: W.W. Norton & Company, Inc., 2002): 30.

44 Ta-Nehisi Coates, "The Case for Reparations," *The Atlantic*, June (2014): https://www.theatlantic.com/magazine/archive/2014/06/the-case-for-reparations/361631/.

45 Hayden, *Redesigning the American Dream*, 59.

46 Sherilyn MacGregor, "Deconstructing the Man Made City," in *Change of Plans: Towards a Non-Sexist Sustainable City*, ed. Margrit Eichler (Toronto: Garamond Press, 1995): 30.

47 Wekerle, "A Woman's Place is in the City," 11.

48 Wekerle, 11.

49 Jane Jacobs, *The Death and Life of Great American Cities* (New York: Vintage Books, 1961).

50 Kim England, "Gender Relations and the Spatial Structure of the City," *Geoforum*, 22,2 (1991): 136.

51 Gerda Wekerle, "Gender Planning in Public Transit: Political Process, Changing Discourse and Practice," in *Gender and Planning: A Reader*, eds. Susan S. Fainstein and Lisa J. Sevron (New Brunswick: Rutgers University Press, 2005): 275–300.

52 Aarian Marshall, "The Pink Transit Tax: Women Spend More Than Men to Get Around NYC," *Wired*, November 12, 2018, https://www.wired.com/story/nyc-public-transportation-pink-tax-gender-gap/?mbid=social_twitter_onsiteshare.

53 Noah Richardson, "Why London's Subway System Leaves So Many Disabled People Without a Ride," *CBC News*, September 3, 2018, https://www.cbc.ca/news/world/london-tube-subway-disabled-riders-1.4804602.

54 Erin Durkin, "New York Subway: Woman Dies While Carrying Baby Stroller on Stairs," *The Guardian*, January 29, 2019, https://www.theguardian.com/us-news/2019/jan/29/new-york-subway-woman-dies-baby-stroller-stairs.

55 Christine Murray, "What Would Cities Look Like if They Were Designed by Mothers?," *The Guardian*, August 27, 2018, https://www.theguardian.com/commentisfree/2018/aug/27/architects-diversity-cities-designed-mothers.

56 Jessica Linzey, "In the 70s, Daring Young Women Created the North's First Public Transit System," *CBC Radio*, August 17, 2018, https://www.cbc.ca/radio/

thesundayedition/the-sunday-edition-april-29-2018-1.4638038/in-the
-70s-daring-young-women-created-the-north-s-first-public-transit-
system-1.4638092.

57 Ila Kazmi, "These Gully Girls from Delhi Are Rapping for Safe Public Spaces,"
The Quint, January 11, 2019, https://www.thequint.com/neon/gender/these
-girls-from-madanpur-khadar-in-delhi-are-using-rap-to-talk-about-unsafe
-streets-and-lack-of-public-transport.

58 *Evening Standard*, "Pregnant Commuter's Fury at Being Forced to Sit on Carriage
Floor Instead of in First Class," February 17, 2014, https://www.standard.co.uk/
news/transport/pregnant-commuters-fury-at-being-forced-to-sit-on-carriage
-floor-instead-of-in-first-class-9133213.html.

59 Damaris Rose, "Feminist Perspectives on Employment Restructuring and
Gentrification: The Case of Montreal," in *The Power of Geography*, eds. Jenni-
fer Wolch and Michael Dear (Boston: Unwin Hyman, 1989): 118–138; Ann
R. Markusen, "City Spatial Structure, Women's Household Work, and National
Urban Policy," *Signs: Journal of Women in Culture and Society* 5,S3 (Spring
1980): S22-S44.

60 Winifred Curran, *Gender and Gentrification* (New York: Routledge, 2018): 3.

61 Curran, 6.

62 Curran, 50.

63 Leslie Kern, *Sex and the Revitalized City: Gender, Condominium Development,
and Urban Citizenship* (Vancouver: UBC Press, 2010).

64 Sharon Hays, *The Cultural Contradictions of Motherhood* (New Haven: Yale
University Press, 1996): 15.

65 Andrea O'Reilly, ed., *Twenty-First Century Motherhood: Experience, Identity,
Policy, Agency* (New York: Columbia University Press, 2010).

66 Curran, *Gender and Gentrification*; Lia Karsten, "From Yuppies to Yupps:
Family Gentrifiers Consuming Spaces and Re-Inventing Cities," *Tijdschrift
voor economische en sociale geografie*, 105,2 (2014): 175–188.

67 Brenda Yeoh, Shirlena Huang, and Katie Willis, "Global Cities, Transnational
Flows and Gender Dimensions: The View From Singapore," *Tijdschrift voor
economische en sociale geografie* 91,2 (2000).

68 Geraldine Pratt, *Families Apart: Migrant Mothers and the Conflicts of Labor and
Love* (Minneapolis: University of Minnesota Press, 2012).

69 Dolores Hayden, *The Grand Domestic Revolution: A History of Feminist Designs
for American Homes, Neighborhoods, and Cities* (Cambridge: The MIT Press, 1982).

70 Margrit Eichler, ed., *Change of Plans: Towards a Non-Sexist Sustainable City*
(Toronto: Garamond Press, 1995); Dolores Hayden, "What Would a Non-
Sexist City Be Like? Speculations on Housing, Urban Design, and Human
Work," *Signs: Journal of Women in Culture and Society*, 5,3 (1980): S170-S187.

71 Gerda Wekerle, "Canadian Women's Housing Cooperatives: Case Studies in
Physical and Social Innovation," in *Life Spaces: Gender, Household, Employment,*

eds. Caroline Andrew and Beth Moore Milroy (Vancouver: UBC Press, 1988).

72   Helen Jarvis, "Home Truths about Care-less Competitiveness," *International Journal of Urban and Regional Research*, 31,1 (2007): 207–214; Gerda R. Wekerle, "Domesticating the Neoliberal City: Invisible Genders and the Politics of Place," in *Women and the Politics of Place*, eds. Wendy Harcourt and Arturo Escobar (Sterling: Kumarian Press, 2005): 86–99.

73   Clare Foran, "How to Design a City for Women," *Citylab*, September 16, 2013, https://www.citylab.com/transportation/2013/09/how-design-city-women/6739/.

74   Foran, "How to Design a City for Women."

75   Prabha Khosla, "Reclaiming Urban Planning," *Urbanet*, August 8, 2018, https://www.urbanet.info/women-land-rights-cities/.

76   CBC News, "Should Ottawa Adopt Sweden's Gender-Balanced Snow-Clearing Policies?," January 24, 2018, https://www.cbc.ca/news/canada/ottawa/sweden-snow-clearing-gender-ottawa-1.4500636; Curran, *Gender and Gentrification*.

77   CBC News, "Should Ottawa Adopt Sweden's Gender-Balanced Snow-Clearing Policies?".

78   Foran, "How to Design a City for Women."

79   Veronica Zaragovia, "Will High-Heel Friendly Streets Keep Seoul's Women Happy?," *Time*, August 5, 2009, http://content.time.com/time/world/article/0,8599,1914471,00.html?xid=rss-world.

80   Brenda Parker, *Masculinities and Markets: Raced and Gendered Urban Politics in Milwaukee* (Athens: University of Georgia Press, 2017).

81   Parker, 119.

82   Parker, 120.

83   Julie Sze, *Noxious New York: The Racial Politics of Urban Health and Environmental Justice* (Cambridge: The MIT Press, 2007).

84   Alexandra Parker and Margot Rubin, *Motherhood in Johannesburg: Mapping the Experiences and Moral Geographies of Women and their Children in the City* (Johannesburg: Gauteng City-Region Observatory, 2017).

85   Parker, *Masculinities and Markets*, 125.

86   Collins, *Black Feminist Thought*; hooks, *Feminist Theory*.

87   Zenzele Isoke, *Urban Black Women and the Politics of Resistance* (New York: Palgrave Macmillan, 2013).

88   Isoke, 78.

89   Isoke, 78.

90   Isoke, 80, original emphasis.

91   Isoke, 2.

CHAPTER 2   **CITY OF FRIENDS**

92   Erin Wunker, *Notes from a Feminist Killjoy* (Toronto: Book*hug, 2016): 117 (emphasis mine).

93 Wunker, 117.
94 Lauren Berlant and Michael Warner, "Sex in Public," *Critical Inquiry*, 24,2 (Winter 1988): 547–566.
95 Wunker, 142.
96 Wunker, 115.
97 Roxane Gay, *Bad Feminist* (New York: HarperCollins, 2014): 47.
98 Elena Ferrante, *My Brilliant Friend* (New York: Europa Editions, 2011), chap. 16, Kobo.
99 Ferrante.
100 Alison L. Bain, "White Western Teenage Girls and Urban Space: Challenging Hollywood's Representations," *Gender, Place and Culture*, 10,3 (2003): 204.
101 Bain, 206.
102 Rachel Kaufman, "Architects Ask: Where Are the Spaces for Teen Girls?," *NextCity*, July 3, 2018, https://nextcity.org/daily/entry/architects-ask-where-are-the-spaces-for-teen-girls.
103 Mary E. Thomas, "Girls, Consumption Space and the Contradictions of Hanging Out in the City," *Social & Cultural Geography*, 6,4 (2005): 587–605.
104 Plan International, *Unsafe in the City: The Everyday Experiences of Girls and Young Women* (Surrey: Plan International, 2018).
105 *Girls Town* (1996) Dir. Jim McKay, USA.
106 Bain, "White Western Teenage Girls."
107 Gill Valentine, "Children Should Be Seen and Not Heard: The Production and Transgression of Adults' Public Space," *Urban Geography*, 17 (1996): 205–220.
108 Bain, "White Western Teenage Girls," 206.
109 Bain, 206.
110 Bain, 209.
111 Bain, 209.
112 Darke, "The Man-Shaped City."
113 Kayleen Schaefer, *Text Me When You Get Home: The Evolution and Triumph of Modern Female Friendship* (New York: Dutton/Penguin Random House, 2018), Introduction: Why Women Tell Each Other, Text Me When You Get Home, Kindle.
114 The crimes of Paul Bernardo and Karla Homolka are well documented.
115 Schaefer, *Text Me When You Get Home*.
116 Emily Yoshida, "Broad City: Meet The 21st Century Comedy Queens That Even Hillary Loves," *The Guardian*, February 15, 2016, https://www.theguardian.com/tv-and-radio/2016/feb/15/broad-city-funniest-comedy-on-tv.
117 Brian Moylan, "Broad City: Season Three of the Comedy is One of the TV Highlights of the Year," *The Guardian*, February 16, 2016, https://www.theguardian.com/tv-and-radio/2016/feb/17/broad-city-season-three-tv-highlights-of-the-year.
118 Wunker, *Notes*.

119 Julie Podmore, "Lesbians in the Crowd: Gender, Sexuality and Visibility Along Montréal's Boul. St-Laurent," *Gender, Place & Culture*, 8,4 (2001): 333–355.

120 Julie Podmore, "Gone 'Underground'? Lesbian Visibility and the Consolidation of Queer Space in Montréal," *Social & Cultural Geography*, 7,4 (2006): 595 (my emphasis).

121 Tamar Rothenberg, "'And She Told Two Friends': Lesbians Creating Urban Social Space," in *Mapping Desire: Geographies of Sexualities*, eds. David J. Bell and Gill Valentine (New York: Routledge, 1995): 157.

122 Gill Valentine, "Desperately Seeking Susan: A Geography of Lesbian Friendships," *Area*, 25,2 (1993): 109–116.

123 Lulu Wei, "Where Have All the Spaces for Queer Women in Toronto Gone?," *Xtra*, November 7, 2018, https://www.dailyxtra.com/where-have-all-the-spaces-for-queer-women-in-toronto-gone-127717.

124 Erica Lenti, "Slack's Closes Just Before Toronto Pride," *Xtra*, June 27, 2013, https://www.dailyxtra.com/slacks-closes-just-before-toronto-pride-50243.

125 Wei, "Where Have All the Spaces."

126 Rebecca Traister, *All the Single Ladies: Unmarried Women and the Rise of an Independent Nation* (New York: Simon & Schuster, 2016): 97.

127 Schaefer, *Text Me When You Get Home.*

128 Jessica Williams, "Foreword," in *You Can't Touch My Hair: And Other Things I Still Have to Explain*, auth. Phoebe Robinson (New York: Plume/Penguin Random House, 2016), Kindle.

129 Schaefer, *Text Me When You Get Home.*

130 Carolyn Whitzman, "What Do You Want to Do? Pave Parks? Urban Planning and the Prevention of Violence," in *Change of Plans: Towards a Non-Sexist Sustainable City*, ed. Margrit Eichler (Toronto: Garamond Press, 1995): 89–109.

131 Deland Chan, "What Counts as 'Real' City Planning?," March 26, 2018, *Citylab*, https://www.citylab.com/equity/2018/03/what-counts-as-real-city-planning/556082/?utm_source=SFFB.

132 Katrina Johnston-Zimmerman, "Urban Planning Has a Sexism Problem," *Next City*, December 19, 2017, https://nextcity.org/features/view/urban-planning-sexism-problem.

133 Traister, *All the Single Ladies*, 73.

134 Kern, *Sex and the Revitalized City.*

135 Wunker, *Notes*, 139.

136 Kim TallBear, "Yes, Your Pleasure! Yes, Self Love! And Don't Forget: Settler Sex is a Structure," *Critical Polyamorist*, April 22, 2018, http://www.criticalpolyamorist.com/homeblog/yes-your-pleasure-yes-self-love-and-dont-forget-settler-sex-is-a-structure.

137 TallBear.

138 Woolf, "Street Haunting."

139 Baudelaire, *The Painter of Modern Life*.

140 Dan Bacon, "How to Talk to a Woman Wearing Headphones," *The Modern Man*, n.d., accessed February 1, 2019, https://www.themodernman.com/dating/how-to-talk-to-a-woman-who-is-wearing-headphones.html.

141 Martha Mills, "How to Actually Talk to a Woman Wearing Headphones," *The Guardian*, August 30, 2016, https://www.theguardian.com/science/brain-flapping/2016/aug/30/how-to-actually-talk-to-a-woman-wearing-headphones.

142 Michelle Hamilton, "Running While Female," *Runner's World*, August 8, 2017, https://www.runnersworld.com/training/a18848270/running-while-female/.

143 David Williams, "A Startling Number of Women Say They Have Been Harassed While Running," *CNN*, August 23, 2018, https://www.cnn.com/2018/08/23/us/women-runners-tibbetts-harassment-trnd/index.html.

144 Blane Bachelor, "Road Biking While Female," *Outside*, May 23, 2018, https://www.outsideonline.com/2311221/metoo-issues-facing-women-cyclists.

145 Jacobs, *Death and Life*.

146 BBC News, "Starbucks: Philadelphia arrests of black men 'reprehensible'," *BBC News*, April 16, 2018, https://www.bbc.com/news/world-us-canada-43791159.

147 "Carding" is comparable to "stop and frisk" policing practices in the U.S. In Toronto, "carding" stops have been labeled "community engagement reports" in which the police stop people on the street or in their cars, ask for identification, and gather other forms of intelligence (address, names of friends, family members, etc.). The practice has been shown to disproportionately target Black, Indigenous, and other visible minority people.

148 Desmond Cole, "The Skin I'm In: I've Been Interrogated by Police More Than 50 Times—All Because I'm Black," *Toronto Life*, April 21, 2015, https://torontolife.com/city/life/skin-im-ive-interrogated-police-50-times-im-black/.

149 Gabrielle Peters, "A Wheelchair User's Guide to Consent," *CBC News*, January 20, 2019, https://www.cbc.ca/news/canada/british-columbia/a-wheelchair-user-s-guide-to-consent-1.4982862.

150 Peters.

151 Clint Edwards, "Why Mothers Stay Up Late," *Scarymommy*, n.d., accessed February 1, 2019, http://www.scarymommy.com/mothers-stay-up-late/.

152 Darke, "The Man-Shaped City," 89.

153 Wunker, *Notes*, 9.

154 Wilson, *The Sphinx in the City*.

155 Émile Zola, *Au Bonheur des Dames* (The Ladies' Paradise), trans. Brian Nelson (Charpentier, 1995).

156 Liz Bondi and Mona Domosh, "On the Contours of Public Space: A Tale of Three Women," *Antipode*, 30,3 (1998): 270–289.

157 Bondi and Domosh, 279.

158 Bondi and Domosh, 280.

159 Kern, *Sex and the Revitalized City*.

160 Bondi and Domosh, 283.

161 Bondi and Domosh, 284.

162 Alan Latham, "Urbanity, Lifestyle and Making Sense of the New Urban Cultural Economy: Notes from Auckland, New Zealand," *Urban Studies*, 40,9 (2003): 1699–1724; Steve Penfold, *The Donut: A Canadian History* (Toronto: University of Toronto Press, 2008).

163 Leslie Kern, "From Toxic Wreck to Crunchy Chic: Environmental Gentrification Through the Body," *Environment and Planning D: Society and Space*, 33,1 (2015): 67–83.

164 Ray Oldenburg, *The Great Good Place* (New York: Marlowe and Company, 1989).

165 Sonia Bookman, "Brands and Urban Life: Specialty Coffee, Consumers, and the Co-creation of Urban Café Sociality," *Space and Culture*, 17,1 (2014): 85–99.

166 Leslie Kern and Heather McLean, "Undecidability and the Urban: Feminist Pathways Through Urban Political Economy," ACME: *An International E-Journal for Critical Geographies*, 16,3 (2017): 405–426.

167 Leslie Kern, 2013, "All Aboard? Women Working the Spaces of Gentrification in Toronto's Junction," *Gender, Place and Culture*, 20,4 (2013): 510–527.

168 Lezlie Lowe, *No Place to Go: How Public Toilets Fail Our Private Needs* (Toronto: Coach House Books, 2018).

169 Lowe, 111.

170 Sharmila Murthy, "In India, Dying to Go: Why Access to Toilets is a Women's Rights Issue," WBUR: *Cognoscenti*, June 25, 2014, https://www.wbur.org/cognoscenti/2014/06/25/human-rights-gang-rape-sharmila-l-murthy.

171 Rocco Kayiatos, "Interview with Dean Spade," *Original Plumbing: Trans Male Culture*, The Bathroom Issue, 18 (2016): 23–27.

172 Lowe, *No Place to Go*, 27.

173 Ayona Datta, "Indian Women from the Outskirts of Delhi are Taking Selfies to Claim their Right to the City," *The Conversation*, February 1, 2019, https://theconversation.com/indian-women-from-the-outskirts-of-delhi-are-taking-selfies-to-claim-their-right-to-the-city-110376.

174 Anita Sarkeesian is the founder of the *Feminist Frequency* website; her critiques of sexism in video games have earned her years of death threats. Writer Lindy West chronicles her experiences with online harassment in *Shrill: Notes from a Loud Woman* (New York: Hachette Books, 2016).

175 Dan La Botz, "Ontario's 'Days of Action' - A Citywide Political Strike Offers a Potential Example for Madison," *LaborNotes*, March 9, 2011, http://www .labornotes.org/2011/03/ontarios-days-action-citywide-political-strike-offers -potential-example-madison.

176 Audre Lorde, *Sister Outsider: Essays and Speeches* (New York: Crossing Press, 1984).

177 Henri Lefebvre, *Writings on Cities*, trans. and eds. Eleonore Kofman and Elizabeth Lebas (Oxford: Blackwell Publishing, 1996).

178 Gerda R. Wekerle, "Women's Rights to the City: Gendered Spaces of a Pluralistic Citizenship," in *Democracy, Citizenship, and the Global City*, ed. Engin Isin (London: Routledge, 2000): 203–217.

179 Barbara Loevinger Rahder, "Women Plan Toronto: Incorporating Gender Issues in Urban Planning," *PN: Planners Network*, July 6, 1998, http://www .plannersnetwork.org/1998/07/women-plan-toronto-incorporating-gender -issues-in-urban-planning/.

180 Ebru Ustundag and Gökbörü S. Tanyildiz, "Urban Public Spaces, Virtual Spaces, and Protest," in *Urbanization in a Global Context*, eds. Alison L. Bain and Linda Peake (Don Mills: Oxford University Press, 2017): 209–226.

181 "Take Back the Night," Newfoundland & Labrador Sexual Assault Crisis and Prevention Centre, http://nlsacpc.com/Take-Back-the-Night.htm.

182 Laura Lederer, ed. *Take Back the Night: Women and Pornography* (New York: William Morrow and Co., 1980). See Phil Hubbard and Rachela Colosi, "Taking Back the Night? Gender and the Contestation of Sexual Entertainment in England and Wales," *Urban Studies*, 52,3 (2015): 589–605, for a discussion of this politics in the U.K.

183 For example, the Vancouver Rape Relief and Women's Shelter became embroiled in a legal battle in 2007 over their decision not hire a transgender woman as a crisis worker because she was not "born a woman." Their decision was upheld by the courts but in March 2019, the city of Vancouver announced it would eliminate funding for the organization until it changes its discriminatory policies against trans women.

184 "About Take Back the Night," Take Back the Night Toronto, https://takeback thenighttoronto.com/about/.

185 Jane Doe, *The Story of Jane Doe: A Book About Rape* (Toronto: Random House Canada, 2004).

186 Carol Muree Martin and Harsha Walia, *Red Women Rising: Indigenous Women Survivors in Vancouver's Downtown Eastside* (Vancouver: Downtown Eastside Women's Centre, 2019), 129.

187 Rituparna Borah and Subhalakshmi Nandi, "Reclaiming the Feminist Politics of 'SlutWalk'," *International Feminist Journal of Politics*, 14,3 (2012): 415–421.

188 Mervyn Horgan and Leslie Kern, "Urban Public Spaces: Streets, Securitization, and Strangers," in *Urban Canada* Third Edition, ed. H.H. Hiller (Toronto: Oxford University Press, 2014): 112–132.

189 Durba Mitra, "Critical Perspectives on SlutWalks in India," *Feminist Studies*, 38,1 (2012): 257.

190 Tom Phillips, "#Cuéntalo: Latin American Women Rally Around Sexual Violence Hashtag," *The Guardian*, May 3, 2018, https://www.theguardian.com/world/2018/may/03/cuentalo-latin-american-women-rally-around-sexual-violence-hashtag; John Bartlett, "Chile's #MeToo Moment: Students Protest Against Sexual Harassment," *The Guardian*, July 9, 2018, https://www.theguardian.com/world/2018/jul/09/chile-metoo-sexual-harassment-universities.

191 Delilah Friedler, "Activist LaNada War Jack of the Bannock Nation Details Her Time Occupying Alcatraz," *TeenVogue*, March 21, 2019, https://www.teenvogue.com/story/activist-lanada-war-jack-details-occupying-alcatraz.

192 This is a trend noticed in all kinds of movements. See Rachel Stein, ed., *New Perspectives on Environmental Justice: Gender, Sexuality and Activism* (New Brunswick: Rutgers University Press, 2004) for multiple discussions of how this plays out in environmental justice organizing.

193 Andrew Loewen, "The Gendered Labour of Social Movements: Letter from the Editor," *Briarpatch Magazine*, June 30, 2015, https://briarpatchmagazine.com/articles/view/the-gendered-labour-of-social-movements.

194 Chaone Mallory, "Ecofeminism and Forest Defense in Cascadia: Gender, Theory and Radical Activism," *Capitalism Nature Socialism*, 17,1 (2006): 32–49.

195 Margaret E. Beare, Nathalie Des Rosiers, and Abigail C. Deshman, *Putting the State on Trial: The Policing of Protest during the G20 Summit* (Vancouver: UBC Press, 2015).

196 Tom Malleson and David Wachsmuth, eds., *Whose Streets? The G20 and the Challenges of Summit Protest* (Toronto: Between the Lines, 2011).

197 Eleanor Ainge Roy, "'I'm Pregnant, Not Incapacitated': PM Jacinda Ardern on Baby Mania," *The Guardian*, January 26, 2018, https://www.theguardian.com/world/2018/jan/26/jacinda-ardern-pregnant-new-zealand-baby-mania.

198 Saba Hamedy and Daniella Diaz, "Sen. Duckworth Makes History, Casts Vote with Baby on Senate Floor," *CNN*, April 20, 2018, https://www.cnn.com/2018/04/19/politics/tammy-duckworth-baby-senate-floor/index.html.

199 Laura Stone, "Karina Gould Hopes Becoming Canada's First Federal Cabinet Minister to Give Birth While in Office Will Set Precedent," *The Globe and Mail*, January 7, 2018, https://www.theglobeandmail.com/news/politics/karina-gould-set-to-become-canadasfirst-cabinet-minister-to-give-birth-while-in-office/article37516244/.

200 W.J. Adelman, *Pilsen and the West Side: A Tour Guide* (Chicago: Illinois Labor History Society, 1983); Lilia Fernández, *Brown in the Windy City: Mexicans*

and Puerto Ricans in Postwar Chicago (Chicago: University of Chicago Press, 2012).

201 Leslie Kern and Caroline Kovesi, "Environmental Justice Meets the Right to Stay Put: Mobilising Against Environmental Racism, Gentrification, and Xenophobia in Chicago's Little Village," *Local Environment*, 23,9 (2018): 952–966.

202 Rinaldo Walcott, "Black Lives Matter, Police and Pride: Toronto Activists Spark a Movement," *The Conversation*, June 28, 2017, http://theconversation .com/black-lives-matter-police-and-pride-toronto-activists-spark-a -movement-79089/.

203 Walcott.

204 Walcott.

CHAPTER 5 CITY OF FEAR

205 Margaret T. Gordon and Stephanie Riger, *The Female Fear* (New York: Free Press, 1989); Elizabeth A. Stanko, *Everyday Violence: How Women and Men Experience Sexual and Physical Danger* (New York: Harper Collins, 1996); Jalna Hanmer and Mary Maynard, eds., *Women, Violence, and Social Control* (Houndsmills: Macmillan Press, 1987).

206 Whitzman, "'What Do You Want to Do? Pave Parks?';" Elizabeth A. Stanko, "The Case of Fearful Women: Gender, Personal Safety and Fear of Crime," *Women and Criminal Justice*, 4,1 (1993): 117–135.

207 Whitzman, 91.

208 Esther Madriz, *Nothing Bad Happens to Good Girls: Fear of Crime in Women's Lives* (Berkeley: University of California Press, 1997); Stanko, "Women, Crime, and Fear."

209 Whitzman, "'What Do You Want to Do? Pave Parks?'," 91.

210 Carol Brooks Gardner, *Passing By: Gender and Public Harassment* (Berkeley: University of California Press, 1995).

211 Hille Koskela, "Gendered Exclusions: Women's Fear of Violence and Changing Relations to Space," *Geografiska Annaler, Series B, Human Geography*, 81,2 (1999): 11.

212 Whitzman, "'What Do You Want to Do? Pave Parks?'," 92.

213 Gill Valentine, "The Geography of Women's Fear," *Area* 21,4 (1989): 171.

214 Madriz, *Nothing Bad Happens to Good Girls*.

215 Rachel Pain, "Gender, Race, Age, and Fear in the City," *Urban Studies*, 38, 5–6 (2001): 899–913.

216 Madriz, *Nothing Bad Happens to Good Girls*; Stanko, *Everyday Violence*.

217 Kristen Gilchrist, "'Newsworthy' Victims?," *Feminist Media Studies*, 10,4 (2010): 373–390; Yasmin Jiwani and Marylynn Young, "Missing and Murdered Women: Reproducing Marginality in News Discourse," *Canadian*

Journal of Communication, 31 (2006): 895–917; Marian Meyers, News Coverage of Violence Against Women: Engendering Blame (Newbury Park: Sage, 1997).

218 Talia Shadwell, "'Paying to Stay Safe': Why Women Don't Walk as Much as Men," The Guardian, October 11, 2017, https://www.theguardian.com/inequality/2017/oct/11/paying-to-stay-safe-why-women-dont-walk-as-much-as-men.

219 Mike Raco, "Remaking Place and Securitising Space: Urban Regeneration and the Strategies, Tactics and Practices of Policing in the UK," Urban Studies, 40,9 (2003): 1869–1887.

220 Amy Fleming, "What Would a City that is Safe for Women Look Like?", The Guardian, December 13, 2018, https://www.theguardian.com/cities/2018/dec/13/what-would-a-city-that-is-safe-for-women-look-like.

221 Plan International, Unsafe in the City.

222 Barbara Loevinger Rahder, "Women Plan Toronto."

223 Moore, "The 'Baked-In Biases'."

224 Fleming, "What Would a City that is Safe for Women Look Like?".

225 Gerda R. Wekerle and Safe City Committee of the City of Toronto, A Working Guide for Planning and Designing Safer Urban Environments (Toronto: Department of Planning and Development, 1992).

226 Oscar Newman, Defensible Space: Crime Prevention Through Environmental Design (London: MacMillan Publishing, 1973).

227 Hille Koskela and Rachel Pain, "Revisiting Fear and Place: Women's Fear of Attack and the Built Environment," Geoforum, 31, (2000): 269.

228 Koskela and Pain, "Revisiting Fear and Place."

229 Whitzman, "'What Do You Want to Do? Pave Parks?'."

230 Koskela and Pain, "Revisiting Fear and Place," 269.

231 Hille Koskela, "'Bold Walk and Breakings': Women's Spatial Confidence Versus Fear of Violence," Gender, Place and Culture, 4,3 (1997): 301.

232 Carolyn Whitzman, "Stuck at the Front Door:" Gender, Fear of Crime and the Challenge of Creating Safer Space," Environment and Planning A, 39,11 (2007): 2715–2732.

233 Hunt, "Representing Colonial Violence;" Leanne Betasamosake Simpson, As We Have Always Done: Indigenous Freedom Through Radical Resistance (Minneapolis: University of Minnesota Press, 2017); Smith, Conquest.

234 Barbara Rahder and Heather McLean, "Other Ways of Knowing Your Place: Immigrant Women's Experience of Public Space in Toronto," Canadian Journal of Urban Research, 22,1 (2013): 145–166.

235 Alec Brownlow, "Keeping Up Appearances: Profiting from Patriarchy in the Nation's 'Safest City'," Urban Studies, 46,8 (2009): 1680–1701.

236 Curran, Gender and Gentrification.

237 Robyn Doolittle, "Unfounded: Why Police Dismiss 1 in 5 Sexual Assault Claims as Baseless," The Globe and Mail, February 3, 2017, https://www.theglobeandmail.com/news/investigations/unfounded-sexual-assault

-canada-main/article33891309/; Robyn Doolittle, "The Unfounded Effect," *The Globe and Mail*, December 8, 2017, https://www.theglobeandmail.com/news/investigations/unfounded-37272-sexual-assault-cases-being-reviewed-402-unfounded-cases-reopened-so-far/article37245525/.

238 Mimi E. Kim, "From Carceral Feminism to Transformative Justice: Women-of-Color Feminism and Alternatives to Incarceration," *Journal of Ethnic & Cultural Diversity in Social Work*, 27,3 (2018): 219–233.

239 Beth E. Richie, *Arrested Justice: Black Women, Violence, and America's Prison Nation* (New York: New York University Press, 2012): 4.

240 Kern, *Sex and the Revitalized City*.

CITY OF POSSIBILITY

241 Brenda Parker, "Material Matters: Gender and the City," *Geography Compass*, 5/6 (2011): 433–447; Robyn Longhurst, "The Geography Closest In—The Body… The Politics of Pregnability," *Australian Geographical Studies*, 32,2 (1994): 214–223.

242 Traister, *All the Single Ladies*, 83.

243 Judith Butler, *Gender Trouble: Feminism and the Subversion of Identity* (New York: Routledge, 1990).

244 Bessel A. van der Kolk, *The Body Keeps the Score: Brain, Mind, and Body in the Healing of Trauma* (New York: Penguin Books, 2014).

245 Don Mitchell, "The suv Model of Citizenship: Floating Bubbles, Buffer Zones, and the Rise of the "Purely Atomic" Individual," *Political Geography*, 24,1 (2005): 77–100.

246 Samuel R. Delany, *Times Square Red, Times Square Blue* (New York: New York University Press, 1999).

247 Brett Story, "In/different Cities: A Case for Contact at the Margins," *Social and Cultural Geography*, 14,7 (2013): 752–761.

248 Story, 758.

249 Caitlin Cahill, "Negotiating Grit and Glamour: Young Women of Color and the Gentrification of the Lower East Side," *City & Society*, 19,2 (2007): 202–231; David Wilson and Dennis Grammenos, "Gentrification, Discourse, and the Body: Chicago's Humboldt Park," *Environment and Planning D: Society and Space*, 23,2 (2005): 295–312.

250 Leslie Kern, "Connecting Embodiment, Emotion and Gentrification: An Exploration Through the Practice of Yoga in Toronto," *Emotion, Space and Society* 5,1 (2012): 27–35.

251 Rebecca Solnit, "Death by Gentrification: The Killing That Shamed San Francisco," *The Guardian*, March 21, 2016, https://www.theguardian.com/us-news/2016/mar/21/death-by-gentrification-the-killing-that-shamed-san-francisco.

252 Brenda Parker, "The Feminist Geographer as Killjoy: Excavating Gendered Urban Power Relations," *The Professional Geographer* 69,2 (2017): 321–328.

253 Julie Tomiak, "Contesting the Settler City: Indigenous Self-Determination, New Urban Reserves, and the Neoliberalization of Colonialism," *Antipode*, 49,4 (2017): 928–945.

254 James Baldwin, *The Fire Next Time* (New York: Vintage Books, 1962).

255 Kern and McLean, "Undecidability and the Urban."

256 Red Wagon Collective, "MAG Art Exhibit at York University," September 11, 2015, accessed February 4, 2019, https://gatheringspace.wordpress .com/2015/09/11/mag-art-exhibit-at-york- university/.

257 Fight for $15, "About Us," accessed February 4, 2019, https://fightfor15.org/ about-us/.

258 Focus E15 Campaign, "About Us," accessed February 4, 2019, https://focuse15 .org/about/.

INDEX

anti-obesity campaigns, 5
anti-Semitism, 18
anti-trafficking campaigns, 5
anti-violence movement, 164
anxiety, 91–93. see also fear
apartheid, 51
Ardern, Jacinda, 131–132
Arkitekter, White, 63
Arrested Justice (Richie), 164
art, 173–174
Au Bonheur des Dames (Zola), 100
autonomy, 112

babies, 27–29. see also children; strollers
Bad Feminist (Gay), 58
Bain, Alison, 62, 66
Baldwin, James, 172
Barcelona, Spain, 153
barriers
    and fear/danger, 168–169
    and feminist cities, 54
    as invisible, 5
    to moms, 29
    patriarchal city planning, 34
    social barriers, 88
bathrooms, 106–111
Baudelaire, Charles, 24, 25
Benjamin, Walter, 24, 25
Berg, Bronwyn, 95–96
Bernardo, Paul, 71–72, 123
Beverley Hills 90210 (television show), 64
Black Lives Matter, 138–140, 174
Black people. see also African
      Americans; people of colour;
      women of colour
    and gentrification, 163
    and justice system, 164
    and Pride Toronto 2016, 138–140
    surveillance of, 94–95, 108
Black women. see also African
      Americans; people of colour
    in feminism, 16

and geography, 17
in Insecure (television show),
    73–74, 75
leading BLM-TO, 174
and nuclear family, 33
and patriarchy, 79
and permission, 108
politics of care, 52
state focus on, 52
stereotypes, 5
surveillance of, 114
survivors, 151
in teen films, 62–63
blended families, 44–45
bodies. see also pregnancy
    and alternatives, 166–167
    anti-obesity campaigns, 5
    comfort, 26–27
    as communication, 20
    design for men, 14
    and gentrification signs, 18, 170
    and iteration, 167–168, 170–171
    and urban problems, 5
boldness, 158–160, 167
Bondi, Liz, 15, 100, 102
Bookman, Sonia, 104
bravery, 12
breastfeeding, 28, 153
Broad City (television show), 72–73,
    74–75
Brontë, Charlotte, 12
Brownlow, Alec, 162
built environments. see also city
      planning
    altering, 153
    and crime prevention, 153, 156,
      161–162
    and gender-free bathrooms, 111
    as long lasting, 33
    not considering families, 45–46
    and patriarchy, 13–14, 29

paradox of, 90–91, 145–146,
   147–148
public vs. private spaces, 149, 160
of sexual assault, 143–147
and statistics, 162–163
of strangers, 145
urban design changes, 153–158
femininity, 102–105. *see also* binaries
feminism. *see also* intersectionality;
      Take Back the Night
   Black and women of colour
      changing, 16
   in city planning, 47–48, 153, 155, 171
   and intersectionality, 16–17
   and Kern, 7
   opinions and violence, 113
   and sex work, 121
   and solidarity, 121, 137, 138
   and trans women, 121–122
   and white privilege, 164
feminist cities, 45–46, 54, 173,
      173–176. *see also* activism;
      alternative visions
feminist geography
   contact at the margins, 170
   and friendship, 82
   overview, 13–16
   and pregnancy, 23
   and safety, 157, 160
   and suburbs, 30
Ferrante, Elena, 58, 61
Fight for $15 campaign, 174
films. *see* teen films
financial restrictions, 83. *see also* low-
      income families; working
      class; working class women
flâneurs, 24–26, 28, 88, 94, 95
Flâneuse: Women Walk the City (Elkin), 25
Florida, Richard, 6
Focus E15 Campaign, 175
Foxfire (film), 62, 68
freedom, 12, 61–62, 100, 102, 112

Friedan, Betty, 30, 75
friendship (general), 81
friendship, female
Black women, 73–74
   and city planning, 81–82
   as empowering, 61–65, 66–74
   fear and safety, 70–72, 74
   interactions in teen films, 62–63
   as invisible, 56
   lesbians, 76–77
   and living spaces, 83–84
   in old age, 80–81
   power of, 56, 78–79
   and privacy, 67
   vs. romantic relationships, 57–58,
      78–79, 81
   spaces for, 66–67, 68–69
   suburban vs. urban, 75
   as threat, 84–85
   as way of life, 56–62

Gay, Roxane, 58
gay neighborhoods, 76, 169–170
gender
   assumptions, 25–26, 43
   and bathrooms, 110–111
   and city use, 34, 47, 61–62
   identity shaping experiences, 8
gender bias. *see also* misogyny;
      patriarchy; sexism
   in architectural profession, 15–16
   built environments, 14
   and city planning, 34, 39
   of fear, 144–145
   and protests, 128–129, 131–132
   public bathrooms, 108–109
gender binary, 15, 110–111, 121
gender mainstreaming, 47–49, 53, 82
gender norms. *see also* patriarchy;
      sexism
   cities' opportunities, 12
   on claiming space, 96–97

ABOUT THE AUTHOR

Leslie Kern is the author of *Sex and the Revitalized City: Gender, Condominium Development, and Urban Citizenship* (UBC Press, 2010). She holds a PhD in women's studies from York University. Currently an associate professor of geography and environment and director of women's and gender studies at Mount Allison University, Kern writes about gender, gentrification, and feminism and teaches urban, social, and feminist geography. Her research has received a National Housing Studies Achievement Award and a Fulbright Scholar Award. Kern currently lives in the territory of Mi'kma'ki in the town of Sackville, New Brunswick with her partner and their two senior cats. She runs an academic career coaching service and blog at lesliekerncoaching.com and tweets about all things feminist, academic, and urban on Twitter @LellyK.